SHEILA M. EI

LATER PREHISTORIC POTTERY IN ENGLAND AND WALES

SHIRE ARCHAEOLOGY

Cover photograph
Decorated jar with omphalos base from Dragonby, South Humberside.
(Scunthorpe Borough Museum. Photograph: K. Leahy.)

British Library Cataloguing in Publication Data:
Elsdon, S. M. (Sheila Mary).
Later prehistoric pottery in England and Wales. — (Shire archaeology; 58).
1. British prehistoric pottery.
I. Title.
738.3'09361.
ISBN 0-7478-0004-9.

Published by
SHIRE PUBLICATIONS LTD
Cromwell House, Church Street, Princes Risborough,
Aylesbury, Bucks HP17 9AJ, UK.

Series Editor: James Dyer.

ISBN 0 7478 0004 9.

First published 1989.

Printed in Great Britain by
C.I. Thomas & Sons (Haverfordwest) Ltd,
Press Buildings, Merlins Bridge, Haverfordwest, Dyfed SA61 1XF.

Contents

List of illustrations

Preface and acknowledgements

The pottery of the later prehistoric period is a very large subject of study and this book gives only an outline sketch. The period covered is from *c.*1000 BC to the middle of the first century AD. For most of this time there are no written records, therefore things found, be they artefacts of pottery, metal, bone or wood or traces of structures, are all the evidence we have.

Pottery is especially important because it often survives when other things do not. It can be recognised by observant laymen as it lies exposed in fields or gardens. Although it is often a similar colour to the earth from which it was made, it is different in texture. When it is gently brushed or washed details of decoration will sometimes appear which are a key to identification and this in turn leads us into vanished periods of our past. For example, a decoration made by impressing a piece of twisted cord could indicate a neolithic or bronze age date for the making of the sherd, or a circular stamp decoration could mean that the sherd was iron age, Saxon or Roman in date, according to the quality of the fabric. This book is an attempt to show how the professional can interpret these small but very important scraps of prehistory and to alert the awareness and increase the expertise of the interested layman.

I wish to thank the Trent and Peak Archaeological Trust, the Trust for Lincolnshire Archaeology and the Mucking post-excavation unit for permission to use material before their own publication. I am grateful to the curators and assistants of the various museums mentioned for their patience and co-operation in answering queries, filling in forms and supplying photographs. Valery Rigby of the British Museum has helped me over identification of the Gallo-Belgic pottery. Mr Jeffrey May, Dr John Samuels and Mrs Cath Turner have all kindly read and checked the text and made helpful suggestions. Finally, but not least, my husband has patiently sorted out the layout and general presentation. To all I am grateful.

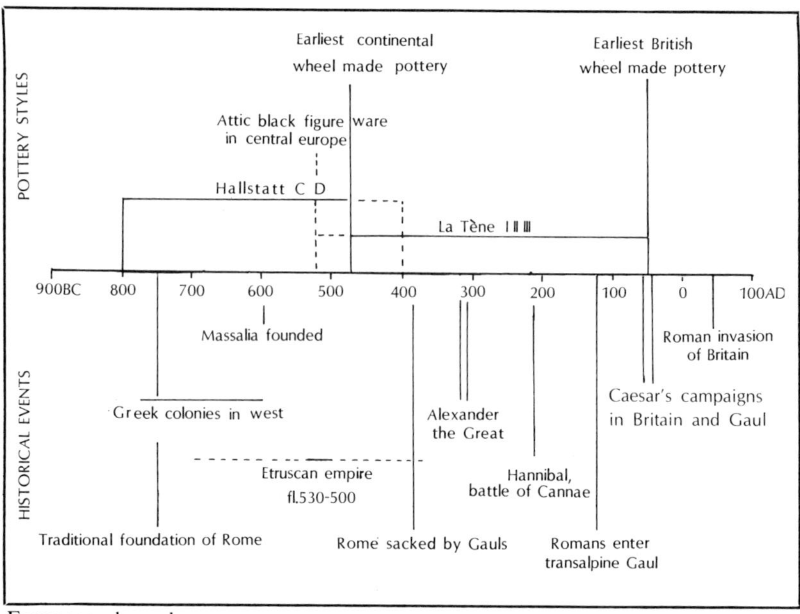

European chronology.

Some radiocarbon dates for the late bronze age to early iron age, calculated to the second standard deviation (see page 15).

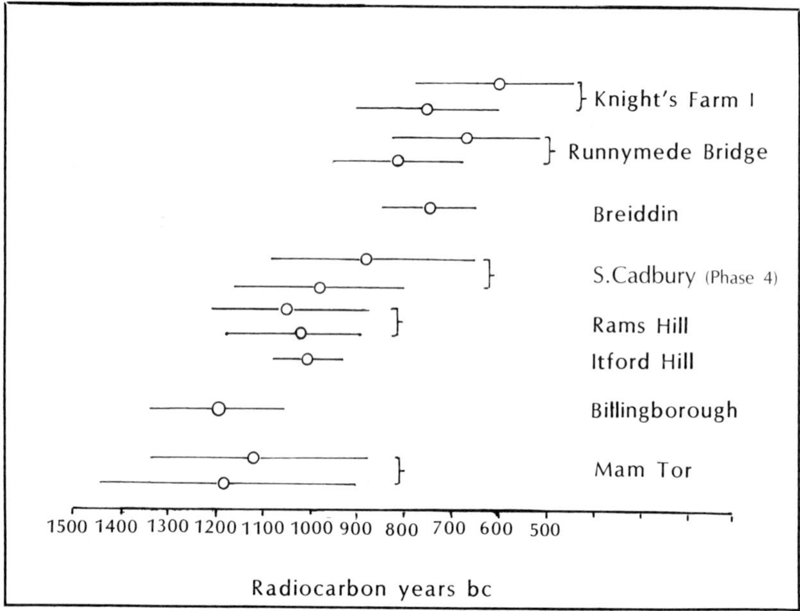

1
Introduction

Pottery is important. In prehistoric times it served man both for his storage, cooking and eating utensils and as a vehicle for the expression of his artistic techniques and aspirations. It is often the only tangible survival to indicate the way of life of the inhabitants of a rural site and the approximate dates of its occupation. Simply looking at it will tell us a lot. The rounded bases with an indentation in the bottom were made to be stable when placed on an earth floor because there were no tables. Decoration is usually on the upper part of the shoulders of the pot so that it could be seen from above while sitting on the ground. This decoration can be very involved and intricate so that it could be imagined as a way of filling the long winter evenings when tales were recited by the central hearth. The patterns used and preserved on the pottery are part of the folk culture. Similar ones, which have not been preserved as they were unfired, were probably used to decorate the mud plastering on the outside of the round houses.

Pottery, as well as being very durable, is often found in very large quantities on iron age sites. Usually more than 50 per cent of what is found is coarse ware, often in very small fragments. These dirty sherds were once part of essential jars or prized possessions used for special purposes. Typologies, such as those discussed in the body of this book, deal mainly with fine wares because, although the minority, they are easily recognisable and good indicators of date. But coarse ware tells us about local sources of clay, methods of manufacture and general standards of living. It is always carefully studied, counted and weighed although very little of that appears in these pages.

For the greater part of the period under discussion the pottery was hand-made locally by the people who needed and used it. It was made both by slab and coil methods, using local clays. At first the potters used their own fingernails for decoration and they progressed to using purpose-made tools. At the very end of the period pots were thrown on a fast wheel, but before that some kind of a slow wheel or turntable was used for finishing off the rims and for decoration. In the first century BC there is evidence for specialist potters' workshops which traded their wares as much as 100 km. We know this both from thin section analysis of the fabric (which ascertains the sources of the clay) and from the fact that similar or identical forms and types of decoration turn up at different sites, sometimes far apart. In this way social organisation and possible tribal divisions are hinted at through pottery studies. At the end of the period some pottery was imported, which is tangible proof of widening trade patterns long before the Roman invasion.

Pottery is found in a variety of contexts. Field-walking collections can indicate the existence of a site and excavated pottery from settlements tells of their length of life and status. Some hillforts may have been important centres of tribal organisation. The distribution of pottery types over the surrounding areas can tell us how far trading extended, the size of an administrative area and whether or not there was contact with neighbouring tribes. The situation is similar with the later large open settlements and small towns. Finally, burials which contain both native and imported pottery can indicate the status of the person buried. Accompanying deposits such as swords, brooches, wine amphorae, imported pottery and silver ware or animal bones can show what needs for food and drink, weapons or personal display might have been felt by the owner of a given type of locally made pottery. The typologies and chronologies analysed below should be seen as a tool for interpreting the way of life of the people who lived and died on the sites.

The first serious attempt to classify British iron age pottery was made by C. F. C. Hawkes in 1931 and his A, B, C division was meant to correspond broadly with the three principal waves of immigration from the continent then in vogue but subsequently largely discounted. 'A' pottery was linked with a possible Hallstatt (see below) invasion in the sixth century BC, 'B' with an intermediate stage and 'C' with an invasion from Gaul around 75 BC by the Belgae, who were thought to have brought wheel-made pottery. Since then dates for the beginnings of iron age pottery have been pushed back to about 1000 BC, direct Belgic influences seem less obvious and the advent of wheel-made pottery is now seen to be later.

Two type sites on the continent form the basis of the interpretation of the iron age in Britain. *Hallstatt* and *La Tène* were adopted as the terminology, named after the salt-working mines and associated cemetery in Upper Austria (Hallstatt C and D) and the rich deposit of metalwork recovered from the shore of Lake Neuchâtel in Switzerland (La Tène I, II and III). The chronological chart on page 6 shows how the dating of early iron age sites in central Europe has been arrived at by means of Greek and Etruscan artefacts found there. Three sites on the main

Rhone and Rhine trading routes are particularly important in this respect. One is the rich Hallstatt D burial of a princess at Vix on the upper Seine, which contained a vase of Graeco-Etruscan workmanship. The second is the more recently discovered princely tomb of similar date at Hochdorf near Stuttgart. The third is the Heuneburg, a hillfort on the upper Danube in southern Germany. This also dates from Hallstatt D. Its walls are built in the mud-brick tradition derived from the Mediterranean cities and small quantities of Attic black figure ware were found there. British dates for these periods may not be appreciably later. The Hallstatt C round-bodied pots with omphalos base and flaring rim find echoes in Britain, for example, at Eastbourne, East Sussex (**5**, 2) and a group of daggers of similar date was recovered from the Thames. La Tène I, II and III chronology is linked to Britain mainly via brooch types. One problem is that some continental La Tène I pottery was made on a fast wheel about 500 to 475 BC and wheel-thrown pottery does not appear in Britain until the second half of the first century BC. This could imply ignorance of the technique or, more likely, that the market for commercially produced pottery was insufficient to justify setting up a professional industry until this time. Some very fine pottery was certainly produced in Britain in the La Tène I period, but it was hand-made. The fine ware angular pottery from Long Wittenham, Oxfordshire, is just one example (see figure 5).

Radiocarbon dates are quoted only for the earlier part of this study. This is because in the later part of the iron age they range between limits which are often as much as 150 to 200 years apart. Many dates from each site are needed from which to extract a norm and these are not generally available. So, while radiocarbon dates are not ignored, more emphasis is placed on typology and comparison with metalwork.

The division of the pottery into early, middle and late groups is arbitrary and for convenience of description. It is based on trends in form and decoration and the introduction of wheel-made pottery. The true picture is a gradual development proceeding at different speeds in different areas. There are marked differences in this development between the highland zone (Wales and northern England to a line from south Derbyshire to the Humber) and the lowland zone (the rest of England including the south-west). In the late bronze/early iron age period, pottery throughout England and Wales is fairly uniform in character and, in the highland zone, these types continue virtually unchanged through to the time of the Roman occupation and after. In the early, middle and late periods in the lowland zone developments take place as distinct regional styles emerge.

Finally, it must be remembered that most of this pottery survived by chance. We are dealing with rubbish which was discarded as useless by its original owners. It is a complicated jigsaw and most of the pieces are still missing.

The drawings of vessels are referred to in the text first by figure and then by drawing number, thus (**1**, 7). A short glossary of commonly used terms will be found on page 59.

Plate 1. Early iron age. Pottery from All Cannings Cross, Wiltshire: (above) a furrowed bowl (**4**, 1); (right) a decorated sherd. (Devizes Museum.)

2
Late bronze age to early iron age
c.1000 to 800 BC

The pottery described here helps to fill the gap which has been left by the earlier dating of the bronze age Deverel-Rimbury pottery (see Gibson, 1986, in 'Further reading'). The assemblages date between the eleventh and ninth centuries BC. The earliest examples are found in the Thames valley region while the Deverel-Rimbury tradition was still flourishing in other areas, Wessex and Shropshire for example. The bulk of the pottery consists of plain jars and bowls which, in some cases, have vertical finger smearing marks on the outer surface. The types found in the Thames valley have thin walls but in other areas these same forms can be much thicker.

There is pottery from *Itford Hill* in Sussex, a settlement site with a late eleventh-century BC radiocarbon date, which may be transitional between the Deverel-Rimbury series and the plain wares described above. Here there are bucket- and barrel-shaped jars with a slip which has been burnished.

The assemblages of this period are dominated by large, high-shouldered or bucket-shaped jars and plain hook-rimmed jars. The high-shouldered jars have short, upright or slightly everted rims as at *South Cadbury,* Somerset (**1**, 1). They can be more angular in profile, as in the example from *Mam Tor*, Derbyshire (**1**, 3), or they can be elegant, thin-walled, round-shouldered jars, as at *Green Lane*, Farnham, Surrey (**2**, 1), and *Runnymede Bridge*, Surrey. There is an example of this form from Mam Tor with applied arcs suggesting handles, an archaic bronze age trait (**1**, 5). The plain hook-rimmed jars are found all over England and Wales and they have rounded, flattened or internally bevelled rims. There are examples here from *Billingborough* in Lincolnshire (**1**, 6) and *Knight's Farm* in Berkshire (**1**, 4), which are both settlement sites. Two hillforts, *Rams Hill* in Berkshire and the *Breiddin* in Powys, Wales, have many examples of both the above mentioned forms, as does the hillfort at South Cadbury (**1**, 2).

A third important form is the smaller biconical bowl with a rounded, tapered or slightly beaded rim. Sometimes these have omphalos bases. The examples here (**2**, 6, 9) are from Runnymede Bridge and they are also present at Green Lane. Fine small bowls are also present, though in small numbers, and a very few of them have handles (**2**, 7, 8). Before the advent of radiocarbon dating, excavators used to assume that the very fine ware sherds they encountered in these contexts must be of a later date. Finds such as those from Runnymede Bridge and Farnham now show that fine, thin-walled sherds can be part of an early assemblage and that not all early iron age vessels are necessarily coarse. Moreover, this does not apply only in southern England.

Usually these early pots are plain, but sometimes they are decorated with finger impressions on rims and/or just below the shoulder (**2**, 3, 4, 5). On one pot from Billingborough there are rare stamped circlets (**2**, 2). There is a rare example of incised chevron decoration on a bowl from Rams Hill (**1**, 7). At Runnymede Bridge, which has dates towards the end of the period, pottery embellished with neatly incised triangles inlaid with white paste (**2**, 10) and sherds with a combed wavy-line pattern were found in association with Ewart Park metalwork. This is a group of late bronze age metalwork typified by a distinctive sword form and the use of sheet metal for cauldrons, which was found at Ewart Park in Northumberland. It is pre-Hallstatt C or *c*.700 BC. Other deposits of this type have been found in lakes or bogs; they indicate a water cult which probably echoed a deterioration in the climate. For a good description of these bronze weapons and tools see Burgess, 1974, in 'Further reading'.

Many other sites which have early assemblages of this type were dug before the advent of radiocarbon dating. Among these are *Eldon's Seat* in Dorset, where there is a good plain ware assemblage in period 1, and *All Cannings Cross* in Wiltshire, dug by Mrs Cunnington in the early 1920s, where there is incised and white inlaid decoration but coarser than that at Runnymede Bridge. The largest of these vessels were used for a variety of purposes, such as storing liquids and grain, and John Barrett has suggested that the production of smaller pottery bowls in the late bronze age could be linked to an increase in the social activity of feasting and drinking.

The dates given here are somewhat earlier than in the older literature and this is due to a series of radiocarbon dates from more recently excavated sites. This in turn allows for some reassessment of sites dug before these excavations. These dates are summarised in the chart on page 6. The dates are never exact and are expressed with a margin of error symbol ±. Here they are calculated to the second standard deviation, which means there is a 95 per cent probability that they fall within the limits given.

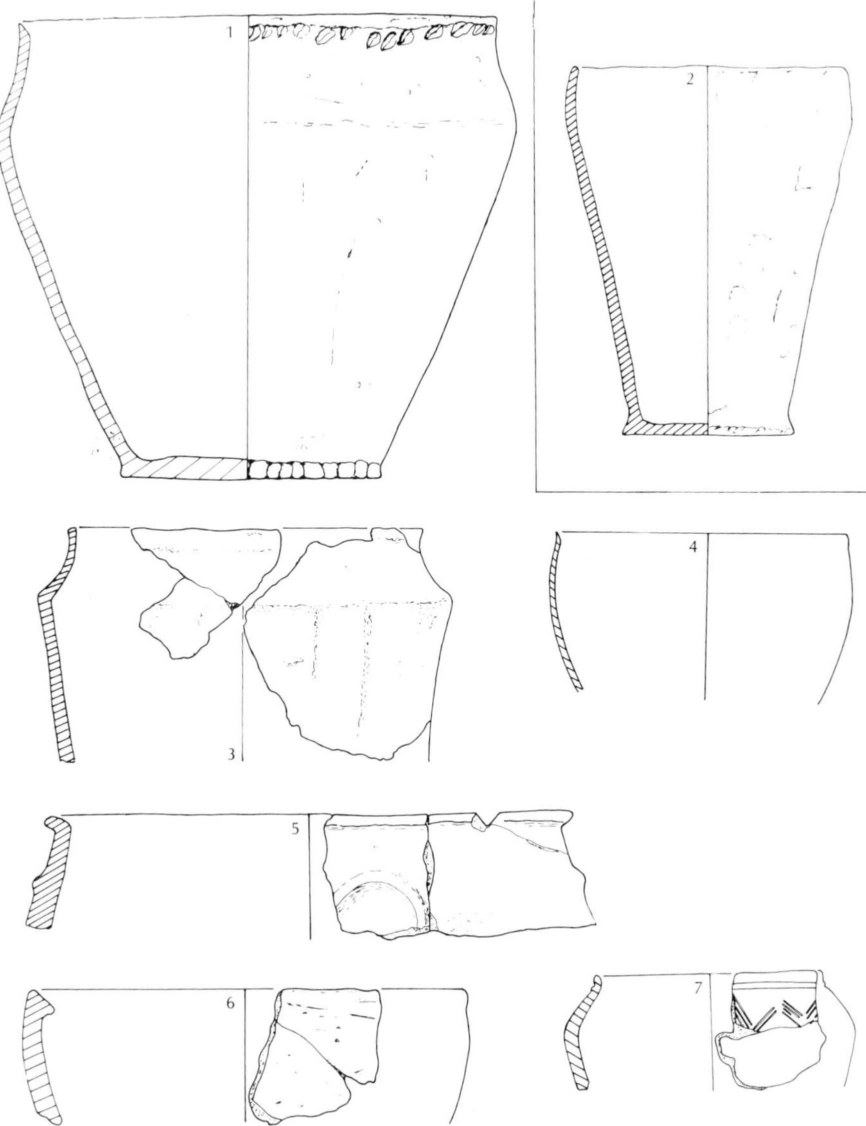

Figure 1. Late bronze to early iron age pottery 1. 1, 2. South Cadbury, Somerset (after Alcock). 3, 5, Mam Tor, Derbyshire (after Coombs). 4, Knight's Farm, Berkshire (after Bradley). 6, Billingborough, Lincolnshire (after Chowne). 7, Rams Hill, Berkshire (after Bradley). To a scale of 1:4 (2, scale 1:8).

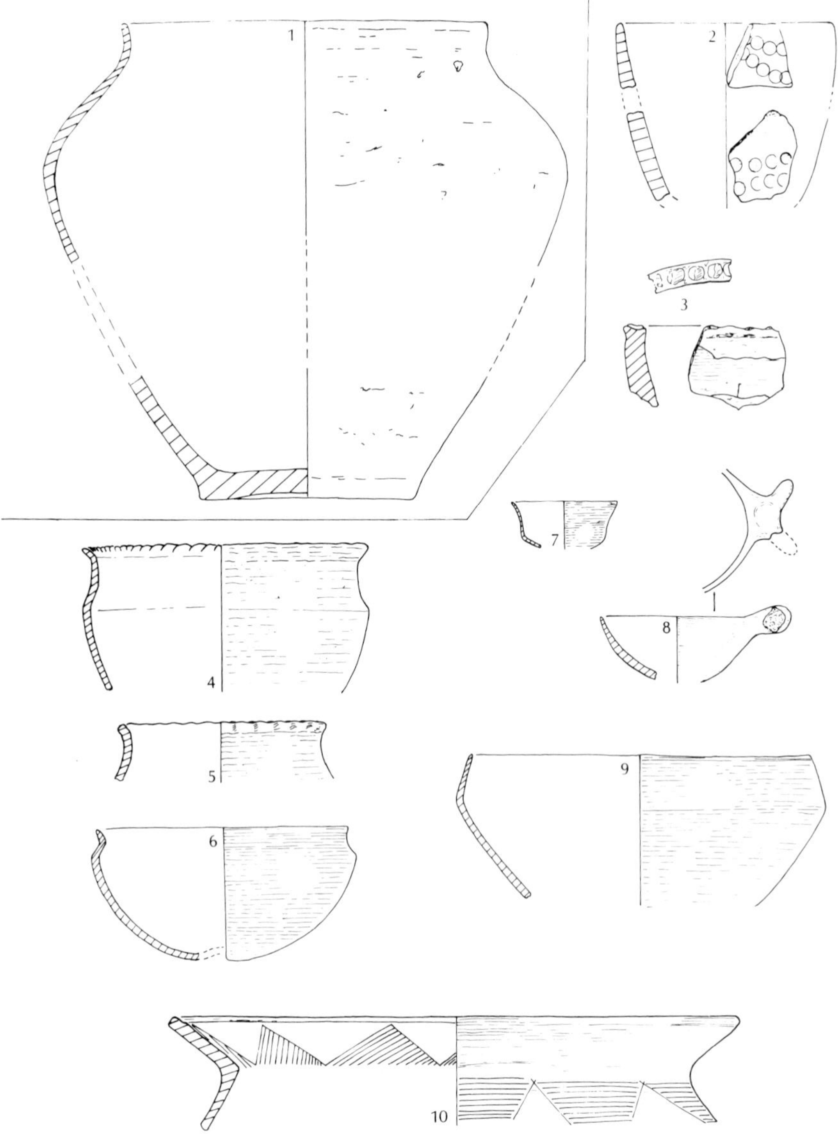

Figure 2. Late bronze to early iron age pottery 2. 1, Green Lane, Farnham, Surrey (source, author). 2, 3, Billingborough, Lincolnshire (after Chowne). 4-10, Runnymede Bridge, Surrey (after Longley). To a scale of 1:4 (1, scale 1:6).

Dendrochronology (or dating by tree rings) is an absolute way of dating material where contemporary timber is available. However, the dates given here, based on radiocarbon analysis and expressed as bc, have not been altered or calibrated to allow for the greater accuracy of the tree-ring dating. Dates before *c.*500 BC become a little earlier when calibrated and are then expressed as BC.

Reassessment (R. Bradley, 1989) suggests that the Rams Hill dates are probably later than those given on page 6.

Plate 2. Middle period. Decorated jar with pedestal base from Eastbourne, East Sussex (**5**, 2). (Sussex Archaeological Society. Photograph: Richard Sinclair.)

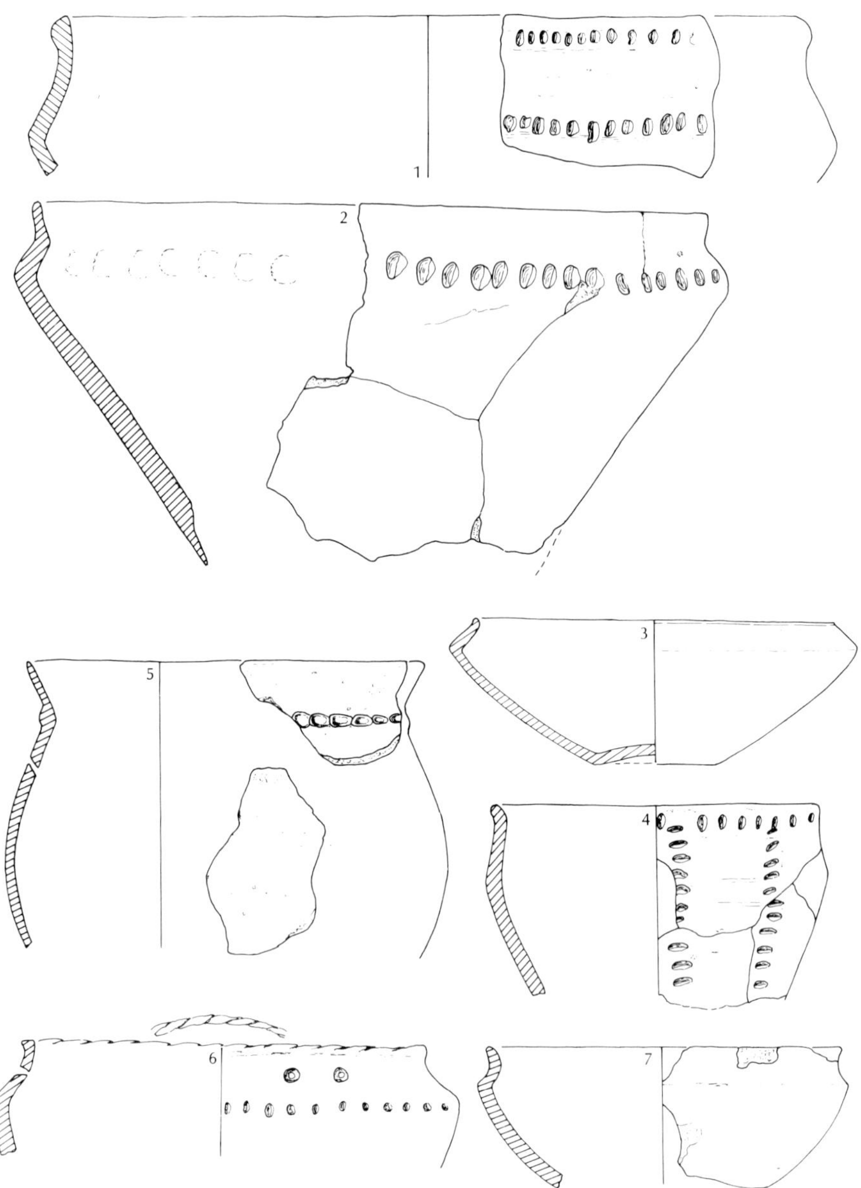

Figure 3. Early iron age pottery 1. 1, 7, Staple Howe, North Yorkshire (after Brewster). 2, West Heslerton, North Yorkshire (after Powlesland). 3, 4, 6, West Harling, Norfolk (after Clark and Fell). 5, Brigg, South Humberside (after May). To a scale of 1:4.

3
Early iron age
c.800 to 600 BC

In the lowland areas pottery now starts to have a more angular profile and regularly to bear decoration of fingertip impressions on the rim and shoulder. In the highland zones of England and Wales, however, the older bucket-shaped and hook-rimmed jars continue in use.

The main forms are large jars and bowls with angular or more rounded profile and flaring rims, smaller angular bowls and fine ware bowls with horizontal rilling above the shoulder. Rims can be flattened or T-shaped with firm finger impressions. Decoration is executed with the fingertips, either directly to the surface of the pot or on to applied cabling. It may be incised and emphasised with white inlay or consist of a glossy haematite coating. The surfaces are sometimes well burnished, probably with a pebble when the pot was green-hard and before firing. Geographical variations now start to appear as the pottery of Wessex stands apart from that in the other lowland areas and there are suggestions of a Cornish style.

Staple Howe, a small palisaded enclosure on the southern edge of the Vale of Pickering, North Yorkshire, has some very large plain wide-mouthed bowls (diameter 48 cm) with sharply angular shoulders (**3**, 1) and smaller jars with more upright neck and rim and finger decoration on rim or shoulder. There is also some applied cable decoration and there are small plain angular bowls (**3**, 7). Angular decorated pottery, similar to Staple Howe, comes from *West Heslerton*, a nearby site excavated in 1978-82. It starts in the ninth century BC (**3**, 2). Dates of the eighth to the sixth centuries BC for similar assemblages in southern England are suggested by John Barrett, at *All Cannings Cross*, *Longbridge Deverill* and *Cow Down* in Wiltshire and other similar sites along the length of the Thames valley.

At *Brigg* in South Humberside there is pottery with applied cabling on the necks of jars with rounded profiles and flared rims (**3**, 5). This feature is common to other sites of the period and one example with radiocarbon dates centring on the mid ninth century BC is a double-ditched enclosure, *South Rings*, at Mucking in Essex. At *West Harling*, in Norfolk, another settlement site, there is similar coarse fingertip-decorated pottery together with fine bipartite burnished angular bowls, some with omphalos bases, all of the same period (**3**, 3, 4, 6). Rims can be tapered, rounded, flattened or have an internal bevel. Features common to this pottery and illustrated here are small holes, usually bored after firing, immediately below the rim and presumably intended for suspension of the pot above the fire (**3**, 6). A group of similar fine bipartite angular bowls and jars together with coarse ware, some with applied cables, comes from *Minnis Bay* in Kent.

Incised decoration in rectilinear patterns based on chevrons, often with white inlay, now becomes an important feature in Wessex and the earliest pottery from *All Cannings Cross* typifies this. There is also stamped decoration with infilling and this represents the fine 'table ware' of the iron age people in this area (**4**, 4-6). Pots covered with a haematite slip which is burnished to give a red-brown lustre occur mainly in Wessex. Strangely, there are no local deposits of this mineral but there are suitable sources from the Loire to the Marne in northern France. Could this represent late Hallstatt expansion? Haematite is applied particularly to fine ware bowls with horizontal rilling above the shoulder, which are known as furrowed bowls. They were first reported at All Cannings Cross (**4**, 1) and have since become diagnostic of the earliest iron age cultures in Wessex.

There is an interesting version of a non-haematite-coated furrowed bowl with a reed-wrapped wooden handle from *Fengate*, near Peterborough, in an assemblage of situlate jars with mainly fingertip and some incised decoration (**4**, 2). Radiocarbon dates here are somewhat later than expected, but similar instances of discrepancies in dates have been noted at *Washingborough* in Lincolnshire, Staple Howe and Longbridge Deverill.

At *Hengistbury Head*, near Christchurch in Dorset, the class A pottery of this period includes coarse ware jars with fingertip decoration, finer angular bowls with flaring rims and incised chevron decoration (**4**, 8), furrowed bowls and decorated angular bowls (**4**, 7). The fine wares could represent the influence of European trade at this site. Eyelet handles are also present on the coarse wares here (**4**, 10).

At the same time, in more conservative inland areas such as the hillfort of *Ivinghoe Beacon* in Buckinghamshire and at other sites in the middle Trent valley, for example, tall jars in coarse ware with upright rims and rounded or only slightly angular shoulders and hook-rimmed (**4**, 9) or bucket-shaped large bowls and jars were still being made. However, their fabric is often good, hard and burnished. Examples of fine ware are very scarce in these

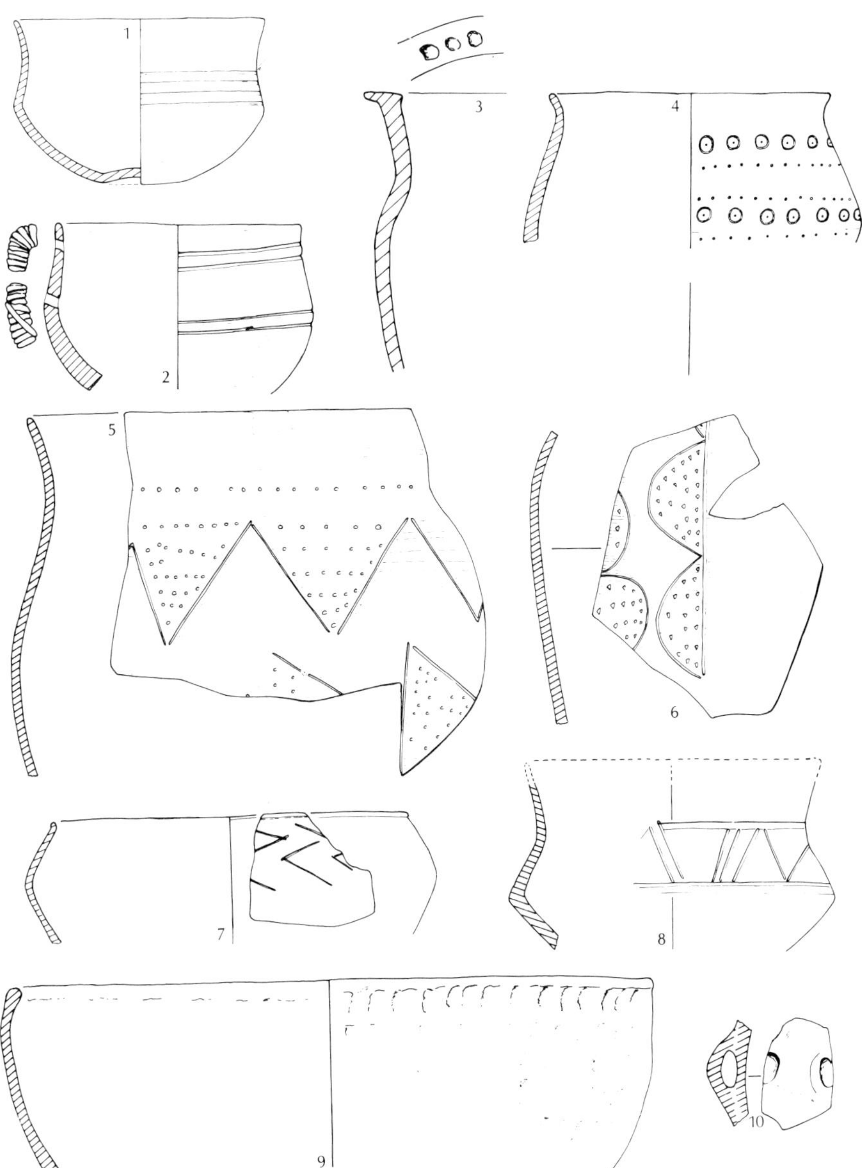

Figure 4. Early iron age pottery 2. 1, 4, 5, 6, All Cannings Cross, Wiltshire (after Harding and Cunnington). 2, Fengate, Cambridgeshire (after Prior). 3, Danebury, Hampshire (after Cunliffe). 7, 8, 10, Hengistbury Head, Dorset (after Cunliffe and Bushe-Fox). 9, Ivinghoe Beacon, Buckinghamshire (after Waugh). To a scale of 1:4.

inland areas.

There is one site in Cornwall, *Trevelgue*, a promontory fort on the north coast near Newquay, where the earliest iron age pottery is attested. These are solid, granite-tempered vessels, large jars of Hallstatt C type with flaring rims and smaller ones with stamped or rouletted decoration of a type found in Brittany (Armorica) at this time.

Thus, while most of the pottery encountered in this period is coarse ware, there are parallel fine wares: angular bowls in eastern England, pottery with incised and stamped decoration and white inlay in Wessex, haematite bowls in the south and the beginnings of stamp decoration in Cornwall.

A very useful assemblage was excavated at *Potterne*, south of Devizes in the heart of Wessex. Here a major open settlement of 5 hectares has 2 metres of stratified deposits with radiocarbon dates. The sequence starts with Deverel-Rimbury type urns and around 750 BC there are large jars with applied cordons and cabling on the rim, together with incised chevrons with white inlay. Haematite coating on furrowed bowls appears about 700 to 600 BC. The full publication of this site should help clarify the sequence in Wessex at least.

Plate 3. Later middle period. Vase from Swallowcliffe Down, Wiltshire (**5**, 1). (Devizes Museum.)

4
Middle period
c.600 to 300 BC

Three forms now become dominant in lowland England, while in the remoter parts of the north and Wales the cruder straight-sided, hook-rimmed and upright-rim jars still continue in use. Two of the forms are new introductions and the first made its first appearance in the previous period. These forms are: 1, round-bodied jars with flared rims and pedestal or omphalos bases showing a Hallstatt influence; 2, angular tripartite jars and bowls; 3, rounded jars with pedestal bases.

Hallstatt characteristics can be defined as a flaring rim and a very rounded body. Classic examples have an omphalos base, but others have pedestal bases. In most assemblages they are recognised by the flaring rim and rounded body as complete pots are rare. These characteristics, together with the presence of hand-made omphalos bases, are a good indicator that a pottery assemblage may belong to this period. A group of three such jars was found in a pit near *Eastbourne* in East Sussex. They were distorted and wasters, hence were probably locally made, but their Hallstatt characteristics have long been recognised. The one shown here has black painted concentric lozenge decoration (**5**, 2).

Models for forms 2 and 3 are to be found in early La Tène burials in the Marne region of France. In the course of the fifth century BC in this region the *vase caréné*, which has a sharply angular profile and a pedestal base (**5**, B), is gradually supplanted by the new, more rounded *vase piriforme* (**5**, A). These developments are reflected in England, where at *Long Wittenham*, Oxfordshire, there are angular tripartite jars with flat bases (**5**, 9), and bowls which still retain, in some instances, the omphalos base of the Hallstatt tradition (**5**, 4). Gradually angular jars with a pedestal base appear, as in the example from *Chinnor*, Oxfordshire (**5**, 7). Slightly later, the influence of the *vase piriforme* can be seen in jars such as those from *Swallowcliffe Down* in Wiltshire (**5**, 1). These jars are undated, but a more recently excavated, almost identical pedestal base from *Tattershall Thorpe*, a defended enclosure in south Lincolnshire, is associated with a radiocarbon date of 400± 90 bc.

The furrowed bowls and haematite-coated vessels which began in the previous period continue in Wiltshire and neighbouring areas, as does the decoration of incised chevrons. These are gradually superseded by cordoned haematite bowls. As in the example given from *All Cannings Cross*, they are round-bodied bowls with a flaring rim and foot-ring base (**5**, 3).

A new type of stabbed decoration now appears at sites on the Chilterns, as at Chinnor, Oxfordshire (**5**, 6), and at *Blewburton Hill*, Oxfordshire (**5**, 5), for example. The new patterns are usually arcs or wavy lines.

In Surrey and Sussex, for instance at *Park Brow*, near Worthing, there are plain wide-bodied bowls and jars with flaring rims and rounded shoulders.

In Norfolk and Suffolk there is a regional group of bowls with angular or rounded shoulders and horizontal grooves on the neck, as in the example from *Darmsden* in Suffolk (**6**, 1).

At *Fengate*, near Peterborough, a site near, but not the same as, the one mentioned in the previous chapter, a group of pits contained small jars which are recognised typologically as belonging to this period. The one illustrated is typical, with rounded body, flared rim, omphalos base and incised decoration in two zones (**6**, 2).

The situation in Lincolnshire is not so clear, apart from the presence of the base of an urn of Swallowcliffe Down type from Tattershall Thorpe, mentioned above. There are angular pedestal urns and omphalos-based jars from *Dragonby* near Scunthorpe and other unstratified vessels which are typologically of this period. Examples given are a small angular bowl (**5**, 8) and a globular jar with omphalos base and slightly flaring rim reflecting Hallstatt influence (**6**, 3).

Scored or *Ancaster/Breedon* ware makes its first appearance as the dominant coarse ware in the East Midlands from south Lincolnshire to Bedfordshire. It is long-lived and continues virtually unchanged until the Roman period in its northern areas but ceases about the middle of the first century BC in Northamptonshire and possibly southwards (**6**, 11). It seems that this pottery may have been used by people of a lower status in society, which would account for its continuance on rural sites while better quality ware was in use elsewhere in the same area.

Finally, in Cornwall, from *Carn Euny*, a settlement site in the Land's End peninsula west of Penzance, a distinct pottery type now emerges which can be linked to fourth-century and fifth-century radiocarbon dates. Here are large granite-gritted jars with upright rims (**6**, 4, 7) and small sherds with stamped decoration which can be directly linked to examples from

Figure 5. Middle period pottery 1. 1, Swallowcliffe Down, Wiltshire (after Cunliffe). 2, Eastbourne, East Sussex (after Harding). 3, All Cannings Cross, Wiltshire (after Cunnington). 4, 9, Long Wittenham, Oxfordshire (after Harding). 5, Blewburton Hill, Oxfordshire (after Harding). 6, 7, Chinnor Oxfordshire (after Harding and author). 8, Dragonby, South Humberside (source, author). To a scale of 1:4. Continental vases from the Marne: A, *piriforme*, from Somme-Bionne; B, *caréné*, from Marson (after Harding). To a scale of 1:8.

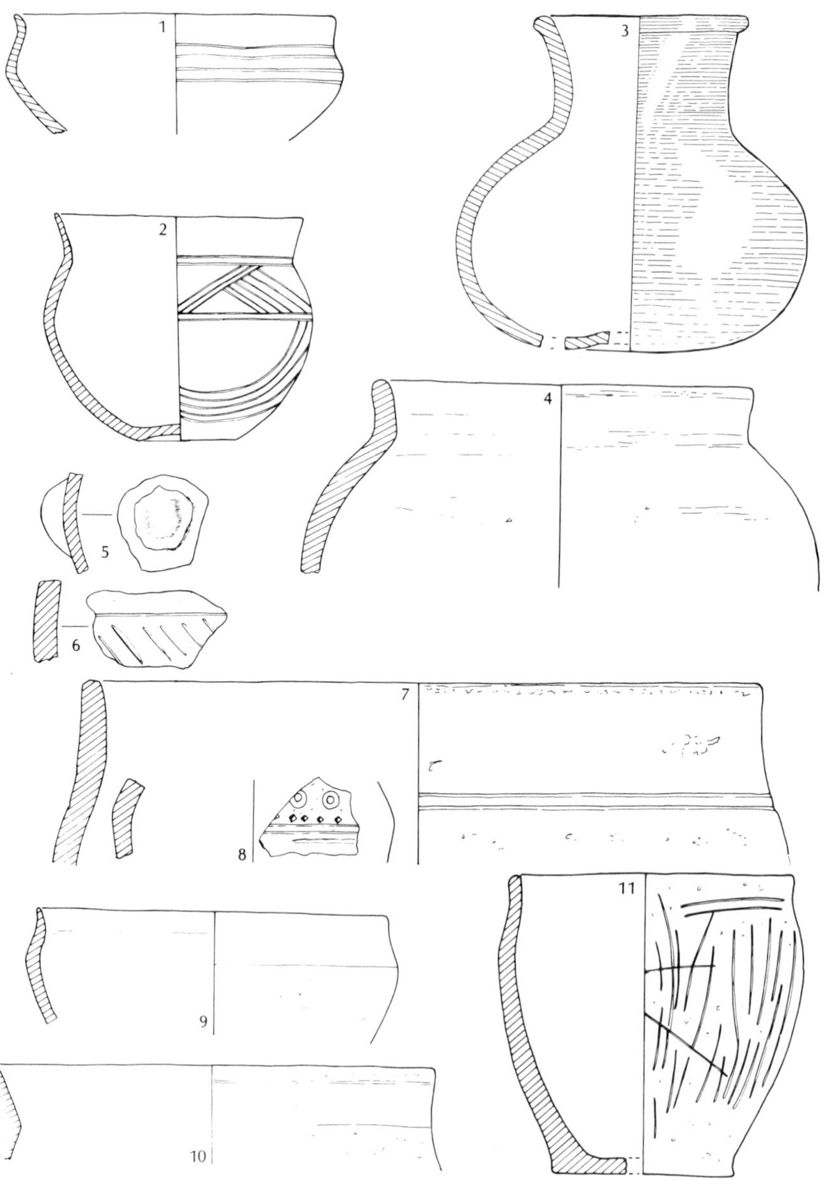

Figure 6. Middle period pottery 2. 1, Darmsden, Suffolk (after Cunliffe). 2, Fengate, Cambridgeshire (after Hawkes and Fell). 3, Dragonby, South Humberside (source, author). 4, 7, 8, Carn Euny, Cornwall (source, author). 5, 6, 9, 10, Bodrifty, Cornwall (after Dudley). 11, Breedon, Leicestershire (after Kenyon). To a scale of 1:4.

Armorica (Brittany) of the same period (**6**, 8). Typologically the pottery from *Bodrifty*, north of Penzance, can now be dated to this period. Here there are also applied bosses and incised decoration (**6**, 5, 6, 9, 10).

Plate 4. Later middle period. Dumpy pedestal urn from Little Horsted Lane, East Sussex (**7**, 7). (Sussex Archaeological Society. Photograph: Richard Sinclair.)

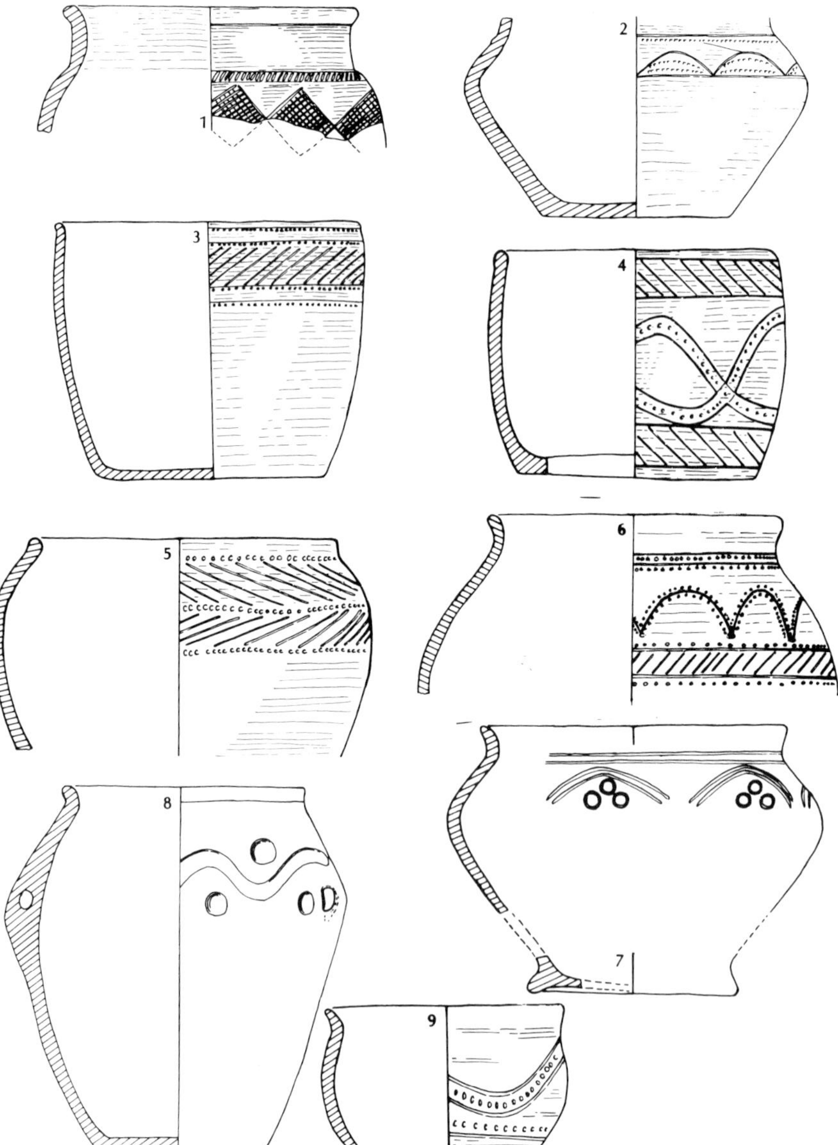

Figure 7. Later middle period pottery 1. 1, 2, Carn Euny, Cornwall (source, author). 3, 8, Maiden Castle, Dorset (after Harding). 4, Blewburton Hill, Oxfordshire (after Harding). 5, Danebury, Hampshire (after Cunliffe). 6, Highfield, Wiltshire (after Cunliffe). 7, Little Horsted Lane, East Sussex (source, author). 9, Hawk's Hill, Surrey (after Cunliffe). To a scale of 1:4.

5
Later middle period
c.300 to 100 BC

Now the pottery becomes less angular and there is more decoration, which varies on a regional basis as distinct styles emerge. This could reflect better standards of living locally while, at the same time, travel was restricted to foot or horse so that inter-regional contact was difficult. The pot forms, however, remain basically similar. Pottery is still hand-made but often to a very high quality and the forms may even have been checked against a template.

In Cornwall the influence from south-western Brittany was noted in the previous period. There is evidence from *Carn Euny* that necked jars with a raised slashed cordon, some of which have an internal groove, are of second-century BC date. Those with simpler geometric decoration, as in the example here (**7**, 1), start in the third century BC at *Killibury* near Wadebridge, north Cornwall. At *Castle Dore*, near Fowey, in phase 1, the simple arcs are rouletted with white infilling, as in the similar example from Carn Euny (**7**, 2). These south-western decorated bowls are often referred to as 'Glastonbury ware' after the type site, a lake village in Somerset, but they are really a group of Cornish La Tène pottery in their own right. Later patterns on these necked bowls are much more curvilinear (see chapter 6).

In the Dorset, Wiltshire, Hampshire, Berkshire, Oxfordshire region the so-called 'saucepan' pots now appear. These are a refined version of the hook-rimmed, barrel- or bucket-shaped jars which still continue in use in the highland zone. The examples given are from *Maiden Castle* (**7**, 3) and *Blewburton Hill* (**7**, 4), hillforts in Dorset and Oxfordshire respectively. The incised and stamped decoration of the two examples (**7**, 3, 5) is typical of Hampshire and West Sussex pottery and is particularly well represented at *Danebury*, an important hillfort in Hampshire, where many jars have a more rounded profile and a double row of decoration (**7**, 5). Similar pottery has been found at *St Catherine's Hill*, another hillfort in Hampshire, and *Worthy Down*, a prehistoric village site near Winchester. In Wiltshire there are also large and fine S-profile jars, like the example from *Highfield*, with a standing-arc decoration in addition to the more common diagonal lines (**7**, 6). Maiden Castle has large bead-rimmed jars with wide scroll decoration and countersunk handles

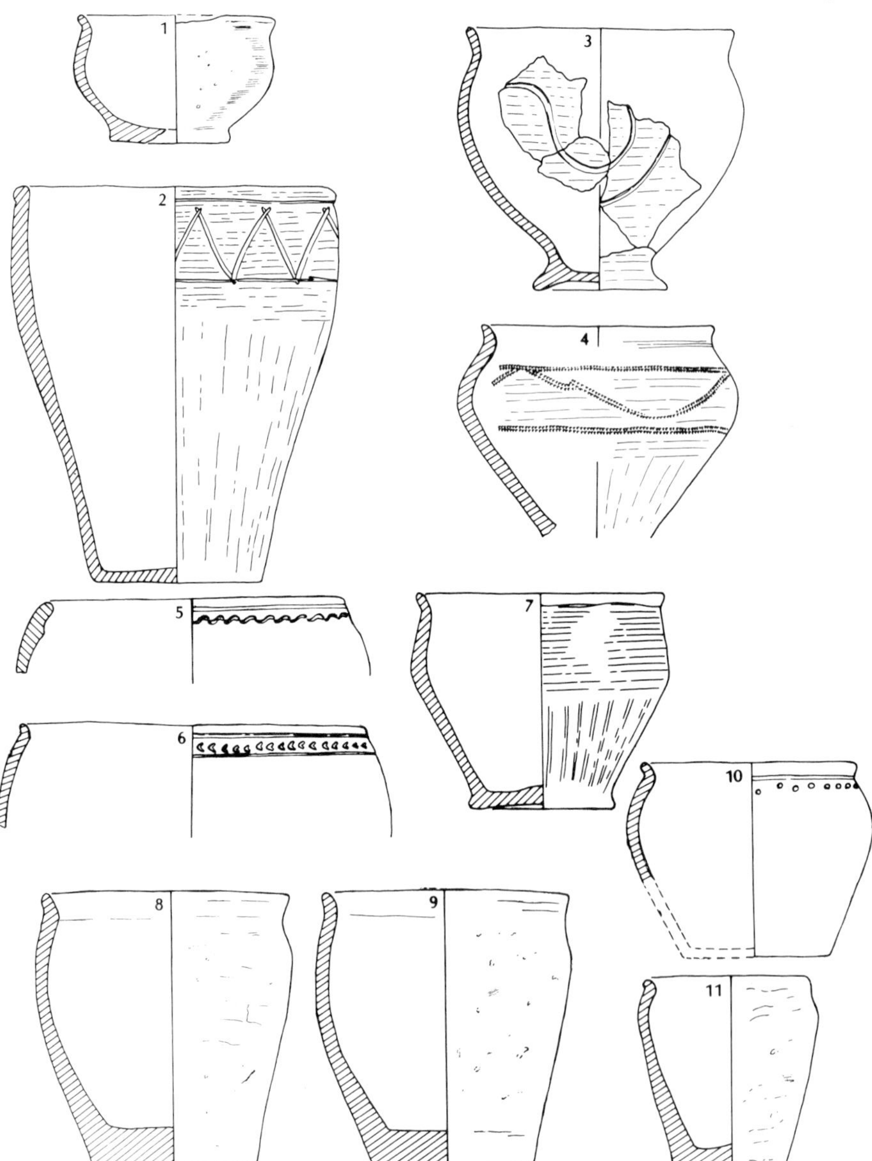

Figure 8. Later middle period pottery 2. 1, Twywell, Northamptonshire (after Jackson). 2, 4, 7, Dragonby, South Humberside (source, author). 3, Mucking, Essex (source, author). 5, 6, Sutton Walls, Herefordshire (after Kenyon). 8, 9, 11, Danes Graves, North Humberside (after Brewster). 10, Lydney, Gloucestershire (after Cunliffe). To a scale of 1:4.

of a type recognised by Sir Mortimer Wheeler in northern France, where they are probably of middle second-century BC date (**7**, 8). This type of decoration has a very restricted distribution in England.

In Surrey, Sussex, Kent and Essex there are small jars, often described as dumpy pedestal urns or south-eastern B pottery. These often have standing arc or 'eyebrow' decoration, as in the example from *Little Horsted Lane* in East Sussex (**7**, 7), or they can have a freer curvilinear pattern as at *Hawk's Hill* in Surrey (**7**, 9) or *Mucking* in Essex (**8**, 3).

In Oxfordshire and Northamptonshire we now see the earliest of the small fine globular bowls, like goldfish bowls. These early ones have a simple, usually rectilinear decoration. The form is illustrated in the next chapter.

In Northamptonshire, Norfolk and Suffolk there are plain black burnished jars of dumpy pedestal type as in the example from *Twywell* in Northamptonshire (**8**, 1). But plain black burnished jars of rounded profile are found in many areas in this period and are particularly well represented at Danebury, while plain barrel jars are common in the upper Thames region, for instance at *Cassington* and *Stanton Harcourt,* Oxfordshire.

In Midland areas the globular bead-rimmed bowls of Oxfordshire are replaced by plain bead-rimmed jars as a common form. There are examples from *Willington* in Derbyshire and *Dragonby* near Scunthorpe (**8**, 7). Sometimes they have some kind of vertical line decoration on the lower part of the body. In the Welsh border counties these appear as large bead-rimmed bowls with scroll or 'duck' stamped decoration, as in the examples from the hillfort of *Sutton Walls* in Herefordshire (**8**, 5, 6). From *Lydney* in Gloucestershire there is an example of a stamped bead-rim jar (**8**, 10).

Dragonby, just south of the Humber estuary, is at about the northern limit for fine wares of lowland type. Here are echoes of the Hampshire 'saucepan' pots (**8**, 2) and there are S-profile, dumpy pedestal jars (**8**, 4). This example has early free wavy-line rouletted decoration. The hand-made globular jar with omphalos base, flaring rim and rouletted arc decoration, shown on the front cover, probably dates from this period.

The final examples are from *Danes Graves*, a cemetery near Cowlam, North Humberside, on the southern side of the Yorkshire Wolds. They are native coarse ware, typical of the highland zone in this and later periods (**8**, 8, 9, 11).

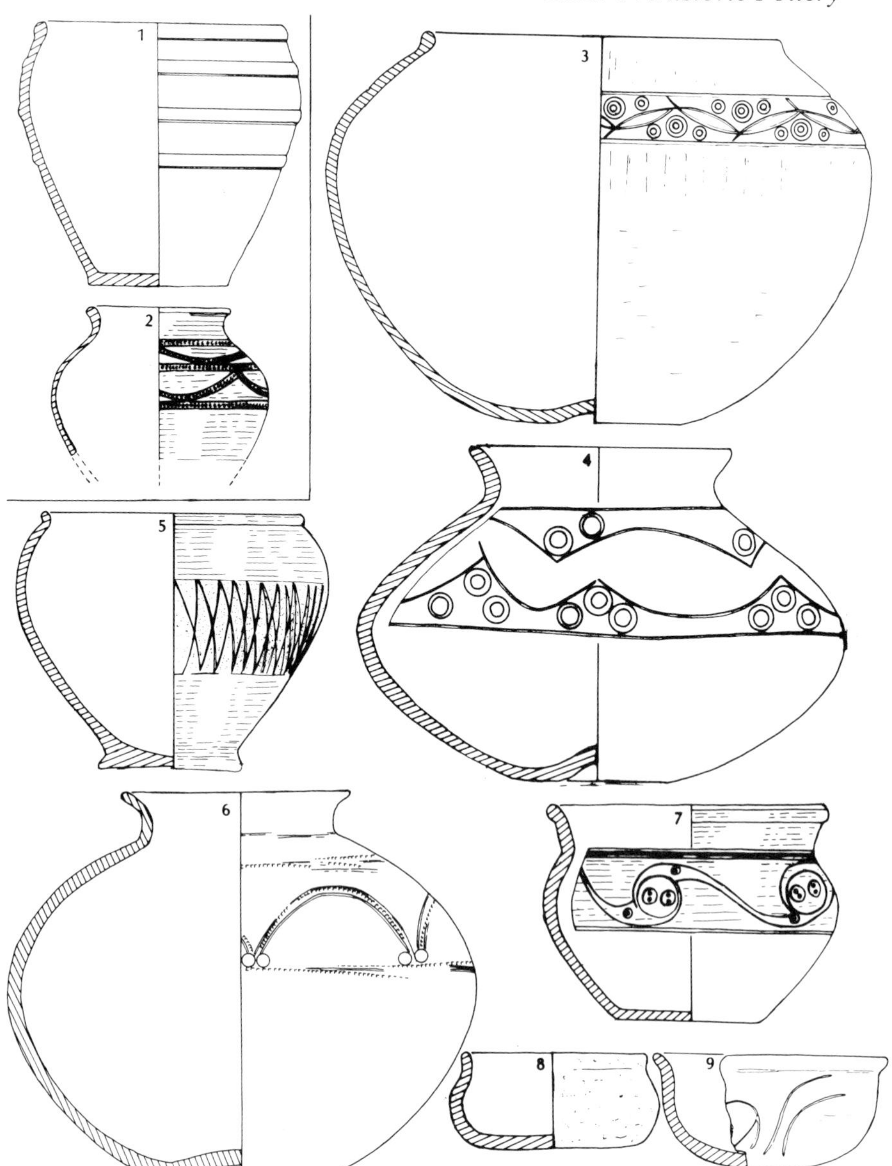

Figure 9. Late period pottery 1. 1, Goldherring, Cornwall (after Guthrie). 2, Danebury, Hampshire (after Cunliffe). 3, Canewdon, Essex (source, author). 4, 9, Mucking, Essex (source, author). 5, Maiden Castle, Dorset (after Cunliffe). 6, Saltdean, East Sussex (source, author). 7, Glastonbury, Somerset (after Bulleid and Gray). 8, Dragonby, South Humberside (source, author). To a scale of 1:4 (1 and 2, scale 1:8).

6
Late period
First century BC: pre Gallo-Belgic

The general tendency now is towards well rounded forms, often with very elaborate decoration. These are necked bowls, rounded bowls with bead rims (burnished or decorated), rounded pedestal urns and large rounded jars sometimes with flaring rims and often, but not always, with omphalos bases. The fine wares are often burnished internally at the rim. A much higher proportion of the pottery is now decorated, particularly in Cornwall and the south-west.

The pottery we are now considering comes more often from lightly defended or even undefended, settlement sites rather than from hillforts. In some cases it can be linked with known tribal names and territories. Regional styles become more apparent, particularly in the decoration, and some of the later pottery is wheel-made.

In Cornwall the distinctive cordoned ware appears in quantity around the middle of the first century BC although it may start earlier. The example here is from *Goldherring* in the Land's End peninsula but this ware is common in Cornwall and is sometimes referred to as Carloggas H and J ware after a site at *St Mawgan-in-Pydar* (**9**, 1). The necked jars often now have elaborate scroll decoration, as in the example from the Glastonbury lake village in Somerset (**9**, 7). The twin villages of *Meare* and *Glastonbury* have a great wealth of fine decorated pottery.

In the Durotrigan or Dorset area decoration is much more limited, usually incised chevrons, lattice or wavy line as in the example from *Maiden Castle* (**9**, 5). The decorated forms are rounded jars with a foot-ring base and the necked jars are usually plain.

Further east are the western Atrebates in Wiltshire and Hampshire. Here we see the simple arc decoration on rounded pedestal urns and jars. The example from *Danebury* has two zones accentuated with stab marks (**9**, 2).

In the eastern Atrebatic areas of Sussex we now find some splendid large rounded jars, often with omphalos bases, and decorated with simple standing arcs and concentric circle stamps, as in the jar from *Saltdean*, on the coast (**9**, 6). Two more examples from West Sussex are in figure **12**: a large cauldron with a raised slashed cordon at the widest point from *Broadwater* near

Worthing (**12**, 1) and a smaller example from *Horsted Keynes*, which has very unusual red-buff painted arcs (**12**, 2).

To the north of the Thames estuary there is a regional group of large, fine globular bowls and jars decorated with interlocking arcs and concentric circle stamps. The examples here are from *Canewdon* and *Mucking* in Essex (**9**, 3, 4). The Mucking pot is very unusual as the arcs are uneven instead of regularly interlocking. It contained a cremation, as did some of the others in this group. Also from Mucking are small bowls with free scroll decoration (**9**, 9). The plain example is from *Dragonby* in South Humberside and fits nicely into the hand (**9**, 8).

Two cremation cemeteries at *Aylesford* and *Swarling* in Kent provide the type series for late iron age pottery. From the early phase come the fine cordoned pedestal urns (**10**, 2) and squatter urns with neck cordons and combed decoration below (**10**, 5). Similar pottery with combed decoration is typical of the oppidum at *Wheathampstead* close to the Roman town of Verulamium (St Albans) in Hertfordshire (**10**, 4). *Prae Wood*, the immediate precursor of Roman Verulamium, produced very similar pottery.

A group of rich late La Tène burials in Hertfordshire contained pottery which can be dated by associated imports. One, at *Hertford Heath*, has plain rounded pedestal urns and concave-sided jars which are earlier than the first Gallo-Belgic imports and probably date from 30 to 15 BC (**10**, 1, 3).

The distinctive form in the Chilterns, which also spreads into Northamptonshire, is the small globular 'goldfish' bowl. This is often very elaborately decorated with a distinctive form of reversed scroll decoration. It is possible that the potters were influenced by contemporary metalworking motifs used on mirrors. The 'berried rosette' which features on the example from the hillfort of *Hunsbury* in Northamptonshire is a metalworking motif (**10**, 8). These small bowls represent a peak of excellence in late iron age hand-made pottery (see Dragonby in chapter 8). The second example is from a small defended enclosure at *Draughton* in Northamptonshire (**10**, 9). Plain but burnished pots in this form are also found at *Moulton Park* in the same county (**10**, 7).

In Lincolnshire, the territory of the Coritani (or Corieltauvi as they are now more correctly called from a new reading of an inscription on a fourth-century Roman tile), there are large jars with omphalos bases like the example from Dragonby near Scunthorpe (**11**, 3, and see also cover photograph). This form is a distinctly eastern type as was the dumpy pedestal urn discussed in

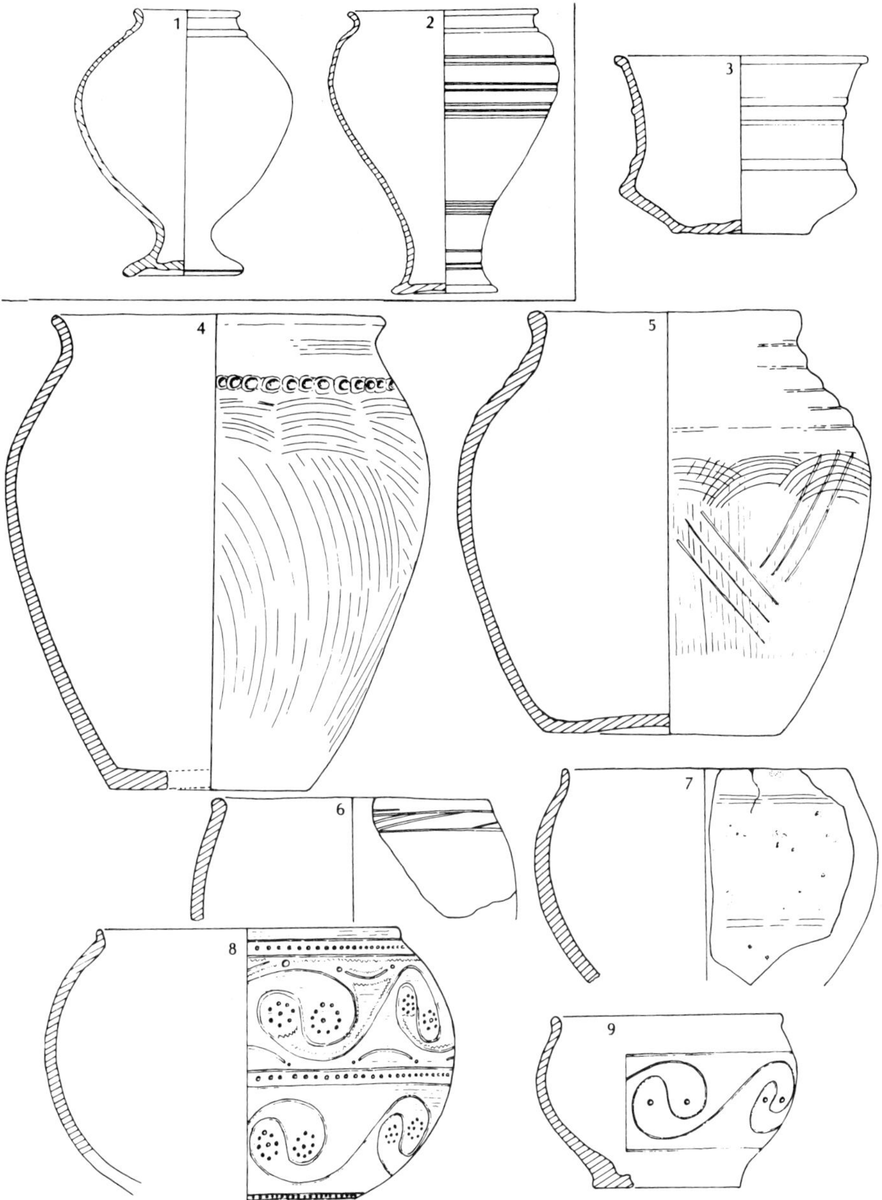

Figure 10. Late period pottery 2. 1, 3, Hertford Heath, Hertfordshire (after Hüsson). 2, 5, Swarling, Kent (after Birchall). 4, Wheathampstead, Hertfordshire (after Wheeler). 6, Midsummer Hill, Herefordshire (after Stanford). 7, Moulton Park, Northamptonshire (after Williams). 8, Hunsbury, Northamptonshire (source, author). 9, Draughton, Northamptonshire (after Grimes). 1 and 2 to scale of 1:8; 3-9, scale 1:4.

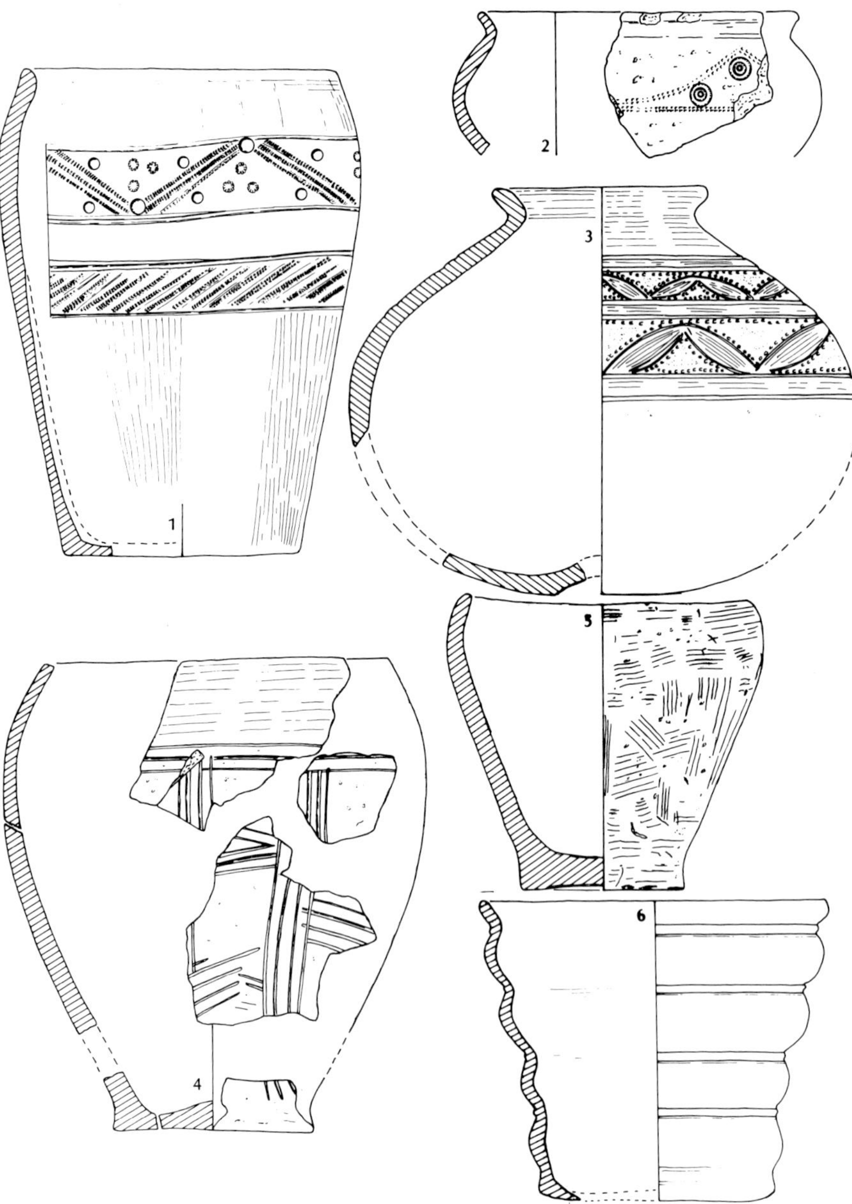

Figure 11. Late period pottery 3. 1, 6, Old Sleaford, Lincolnshire (source, author). 2, 3, Dragonby, South Humberside (source, author). 4, Fisherwick, Staffordshire (source, author). 5, Catcote, Cleveland (after Challis and Harding). To a scale of 1:4.

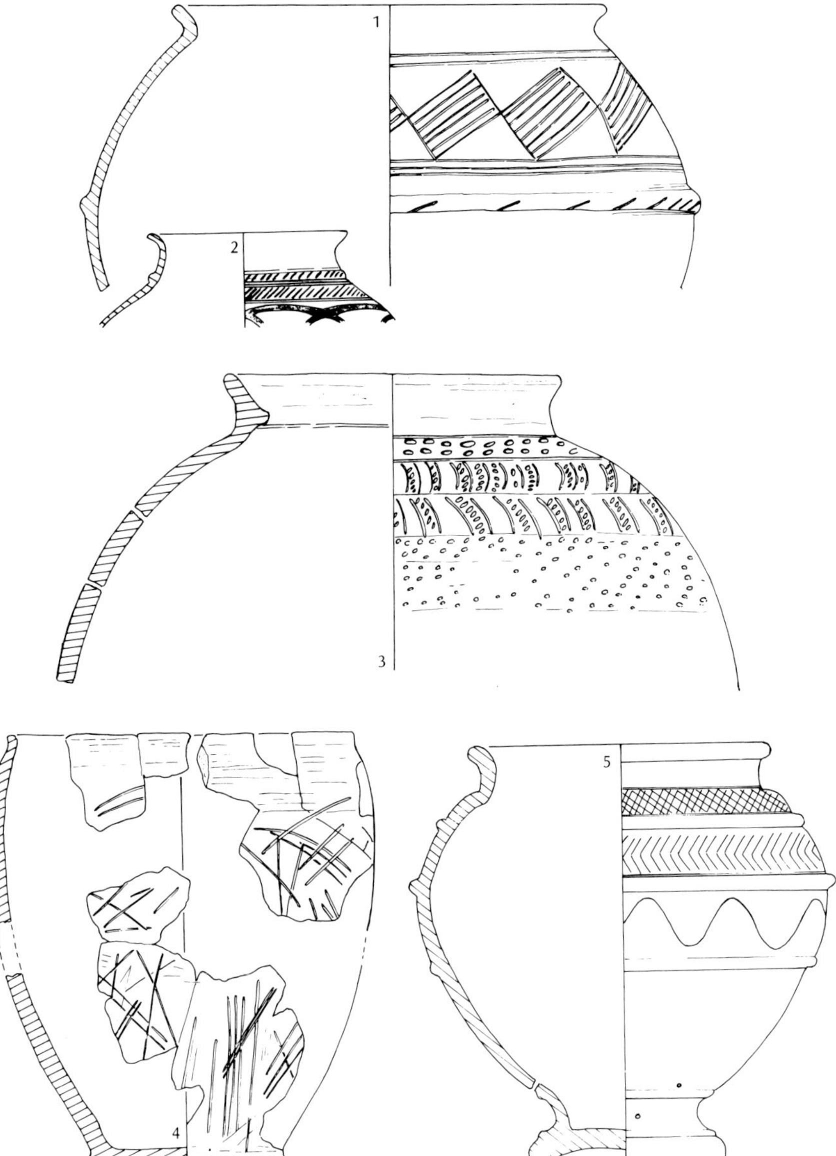

Figure 12. Late period pottery 4. 1, Broadwater, West Sussex (after Cunliffe). 2, Horsted Keynes, West Sussex (after Cunliffe). 3, Carn Euny, Cornwall (source, author). 4, Holme Pierrepont, Nottinghamshire (source, author). 5, Dragonby, South Humberside (source, author). To a scale of 1:6.

Plate 5. Late period. Bowl from Canewdon, Essex (**9**, 3). (Southend Museum Service.)
Plate 6. Late period. Bowl from Hunsbury hillfort, Northamptonshire (**10**, 8). (Northampton Borough Council.)

the previous chapter. Examples of these large jars are illustrated from Saltdean in East Sussex (**9**, 6) and Mucking in Essex (**9**, 4). At Dragonby the interlocking arcs of Sussex and Essex are repeated. Also from Dragonby come small bowls with free curvilinear decoration and circular stamps (**11**, 2). From excavations at *Old Sleaford* there is a barrel jar with rouletted chevron and stamped decoration (**11**, 1) and a handmade corrugated jar similar again to examples from Kent and Essex (**11**, 6). Several fine wheel-made jars with neck cordons, similar to those from Dragonby, were found in 1987 at *Brantingham*, near Hull, North Humberside, and at *Risby* and *Bursea* a little to the west, near the river Foulness. This is the most northerly point so far recorded for this fine native late iron age pottery.

In Herefordshire and the Welsh borders, in the first century BC, a new kind of decoration gradually replaces the 'duck stamps' on the large bead-rimmed barrel jars. The new patterns are diagonal lines, chevrons and lattice patterns, as in the example from *Midsummer Hill* (**10**, 6). They could reflect the presence of newcomers in the region and certainly indicate new influences.

In the more rural area of the East Midlands, Derbyshire, south Nottinghamshire and Leicestershire, the scored wares continue and overlap with the wheel-made pottery. The fabric becomes fine and hard, as at *Holme Pierrepont* near Nottingham (**12**, 4), and the scoring can be organised into a pattern, as at *Fisherwick* in Staffordshire (**11**, 4).

Meanwhile in the Yorkshire and Durham areas pottery is still primitive in the plain open jar tradition, as at *Catcote*, near Hartlepool, Cleveland (**11**, 5). In the Brigantian territories further north there is very little pottery before the first century AD. In the remoter parts of Wales too there is very little pottery of any kind at this period.

Throughout the lowland zone very large fine cauldrons now appear in the potter's repertoire. The examples in figure 12 come from Cornwall (**12**, 3), West Sussex (**12**, 1) and South Humberside (**12**, 5). The one from Dragonby (**12**, 5) is not only complete but has been carefully repaired in antiquity. They must have been valued pieces, probably for some alcoholic drink which formed a central part of feasts.

Plate 7. (Above) Late period. Cremation urn from Mucking, Essex (**9**, 4). (British Museum. Photograph: W. T. Jones.)

Plate 8. (Right) Late period. Stamp-decorated jar from Old Sleaford, Lincolnshire (**11**, 1). (Trust for Lincolnshire Archaeology. Photograph: P. Dixon.)

7
Very late pottery
c.15-10 BC to first decades of Roman occupation

The very latest iron age pottery in Britain can often be defined by the presence or absence of Gallo-Belgic pottery in the assemblage, so it is useful to be able to recognise some of the basic forms and fabrics. This very fine wheel-made pottery was manufactured in Gallia Belgica, that is north-eastern France and the Low Countries. It was developed specifically to supply the Roman armies of occupation and it came to Britain by way of trade. It can be quite closely dated by its presence or absence from Roman forts, where the dates of occupation are historically attested, such as Haltern and Oberaden on the river Lippe, an eastern tributary of the Rhine. Oberaden was abandoned about 11 to 9 BC, with the death of Drusus, and Haltern flourished from 8 BC to AD 9. These forts give a starting date for this pottery, which was modelled on the Roman light-red Arretine ware. Other forts, such as Hofheim and Nijmegen, give a chronology for Gallo-Belgic pottery through the Augustan, Tiberian and Claudian periods until its eventual decline at the beginning of the Flavian period in about AD 69. Considerable quantities of Gallo-Belgic pottery were imported into Britain in the decades before the invasion of Claudius in AD 43 and most authorities accept that there is probably not much of a time gap between the continental dates and dates of export to Britain, where it is found throughout the lowland zone from Lincolnshire to Cornwall, although it is commoner in the south-east.

True Gallo-Belgic pottery comes in two fabrics: red or Terra Rubra (TR) and black or Terra Nigra (TN). The TN is a very fine light-grey ware with black to light grey polished surfaces which sometimes have a coating of mica. Both wares are instantly recognisable even in small sherds. The forms are platters, cups and beakers as in the selection given in figure 13. The forms were first categorised at *Camulodunum* (Colchester, Essex) in 1947 and, although they have been much refined since then, the CAM numbers are still widely used as a basic reference. (An assessment can be found in the report on Skeleton Green by Valery Rigby, 1981.) Many of the forms occur in both TN and TR, the TR versions being the earlier. The CAM 2 platters (**13**, 2) are amongst the earliest common forms, usually pre-conquest and in highly polished TN. The CAM 5 platters are commonly found and they are dated *c*.10 BC to AD 60. 65 per cent of them are in TN and 35 per cent in TR. CAM 5A (**13**, 3) is usually large and changes little over the time span. They may have rouletted circles inside as in the example from *Skeleton Green* (**13**, 1). These early forms have not so far been found north of Leicester. The CAM 8 and 56 (**13**, 4, 5) make a set of cup and platter and are dated AD 20 to 65; CAM 56C (**13**, 4) is in TN. The CAM 16 platters (**13**, 6) in TN, with the raised centres, are the latest of the platters at *c*.AD 60 to 85. These forms are widely imitated in local fabrics and the dates are relatively later; thus, for example, CAM 26 (**13**, 7) is a copy of the Claudian CAM 12 and CAM 30 (**13**, 8) is a copy of the post-conquest CAM 16 (**13**, 6). The CAM 51 (**13**, 9) are so called 'bobbin beakers' in micaceous black ware; they are usually pre-conquest. The CAM 76A beakers (**13**, 10) are in a dark orange version of TR and are highly polished, with a date range of 10 BC to AD 10. This form and similar ones are widely imitated in the Flavian period.

A third kind of instantly recognisable and diagnostic ware found frequently is the fine white or pinkish fabric of the butt beakers, which were probably some kind of specialised drinking vessel. The earliest forms started about 10 BC but the most commonly found is the CAM 113 with its rim undercut internally (**13**, 11). This form is very common at Camulodunum up to *c*.AD 60. There are many imitations in local fabric in the Flavian period as the beaker was clearly an important and popular vessel. Flagons such as CAM 136A (**13**, 12) and two-handled jugs were made in white ware but much thicker than the butt-beaker fabric. This, too, is easily recognisable and some of the earliest examples were found in a rich cremation burial at *Lexden* in Essex dated not very long before the Roman conquest. The final type of imported vessel found in the late iron age is the large Roman amphora of Dressel types 1 A and B. They were made in Italy in the first half of the first century BC and were imported full of wine. Most of them were found in the group of rich cremation burials in Hertfordshire but they do occur elsewhere. Even small sherds are easily identified as they are very thick and their origin can easily be determined by petrological analysis.

With all this independent dating evidence it is comparatively easy to isolate the very late iron age pottery forms, some of which continued to be made with increasing skill until several decades after the Roman conquest. All the pottery is now wheel-made except in the remotest regions and this makes for a high degree of consistency in the shapes. Many jars have cordons, sometimes

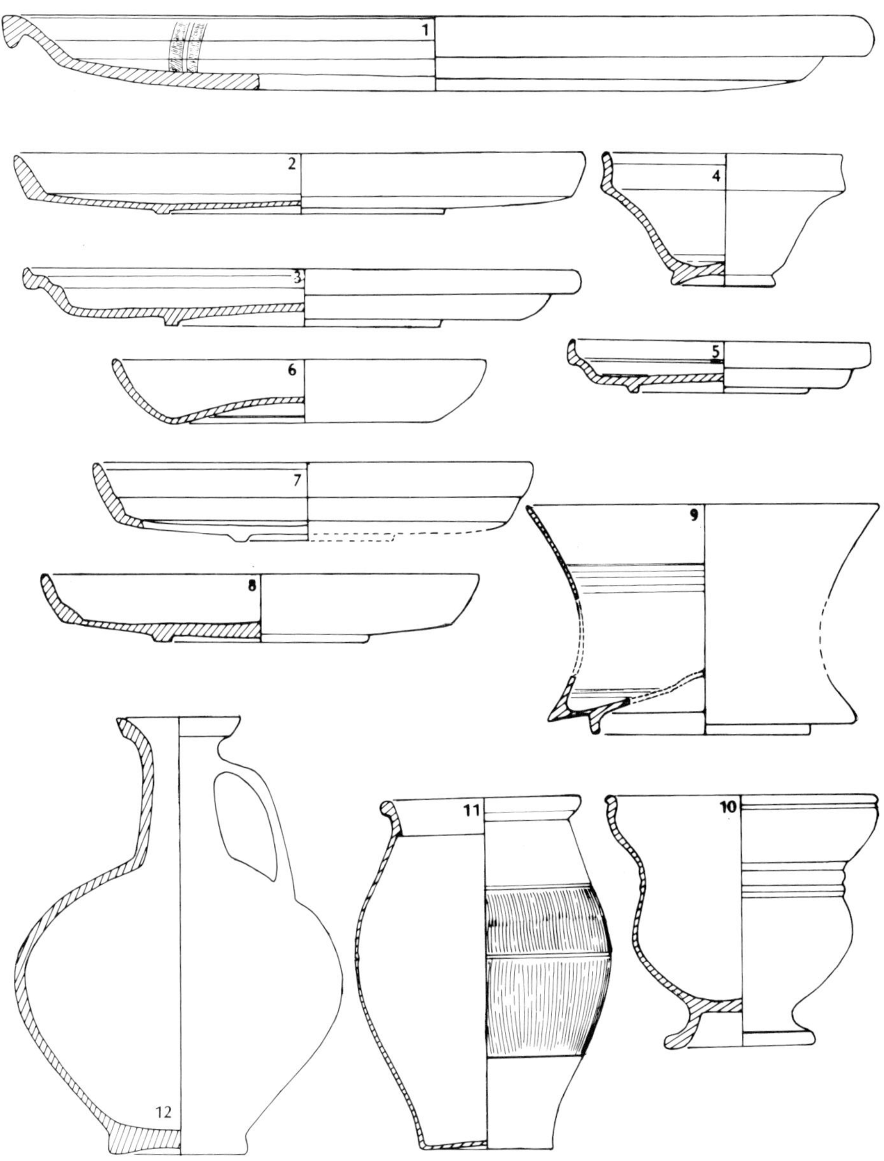

Figure 13. Gallo-Belgic pottery and imitations. 1, Skeleton Green, Hertfordshire, form 20a (after Rigby). 2-12, Camulodunum, Essex (after Hawkes and Hull): 2, CAM 2B; 3, CAM 5A; 4, CAM 56C; 5, CAM 8; 6, CAM 16A; 7, CAM 26; 8, CAM 30; 9, CAM 51C; 10, CAM 76A; 11, CAM 113; 12, CAM 136A. To a scale of 1:4.

over the whole body (**15**, 3, 6), and the decoration, generally less in evidence, is modified to fit them (**14**, 1, 2). There are many small concave-sided bowls in fine ware with cordons at the waist (**14**, 9, and **15**, 4); small-necked jars in fine plain fabric are very common (**15**, 5), as are imitation butt beakers (**14**, 6) and both plain and decorated bead-rim globular and ovoid jars (**14**, 5, and **15**, 2). Among the coarse wares, the great roll-rimmed jars are typical of this period, sometimes with combed decoration (**15**, 1) or with a row of crude stamps in a flat cordon (**18**, 15, 16).

In parallel with the changes in pottery styles and techniques, the sites are now also much more clearly defined. Some are very large open settlements or small towns (oppida) such as Camulodonum (Colchester, Essex), *Braughing* (Skeleton Green), *Baldock* and *Verulamium* (Hertfordshire), *Dragonby* (South Humberside) and *Old Sleaford* (Lincolnshire). All of these became Roman towns. Others are hillforts and oppida re-fortified in their final stages, as at *Danebury* (Hampshire), *Bagendon* (Gloucestershire) and *Maiden Castle* (Dorset). In Cornwall they are villages with stone-built round houses such as *Carn Euny* and *Carloggas*. The last category is cremation cemeteries as at *Aylesford* and *Swarling* in Kent and rich single burials at *Welwyn* and *Hertford Heath* in Hertfordshire and Lexden (Essex), for example.

Quantities of pottery in this period are very large and it is possible here only to point to a few of the most typical forms. At *Dragonby*, South Humberside, where the assemblage has been extensively studied, the very latest native iron age forms include bead-rim globular and ovoid jars, tall jars with flared rims, necked bowls and jars with tooled lattice decoration in narrow bands (**14**, 2), concave-sided bowls with waist cordons (as **14**, 9) and beakers and larger jars with zones of decoration on flat cordons often in direct imitation of butt beakers (as **14**, 6, from Aylesford). These forms and features are echoed at many other sites. At *Old Sleaford* and nearby *Ancaster*, Lincolnshire, the fine-necked jars still have rouletted decoration but it is compressed into narrow cordons (**14**, 1). Also typical here are ovoid jars with zones of combed decoration and one to six perforations in the base (**15**, 2). At *Danebury* a large collection of pottery includes pedestal urns, jars and bowls with incised decoration (**14**, 3, 5) and numerous imitation butt beakers. At *Hengistbury Head*, Dorset, there is a class of fine late cordoned jars (**15**, 6).

At *Skeleton Green* there are large jars with multiple cordons at the neck (**15**, 3) and the typical large storage jars (**15**, 1). At *Baldock*, in addition to the common small-necked jar (**15**, 5),

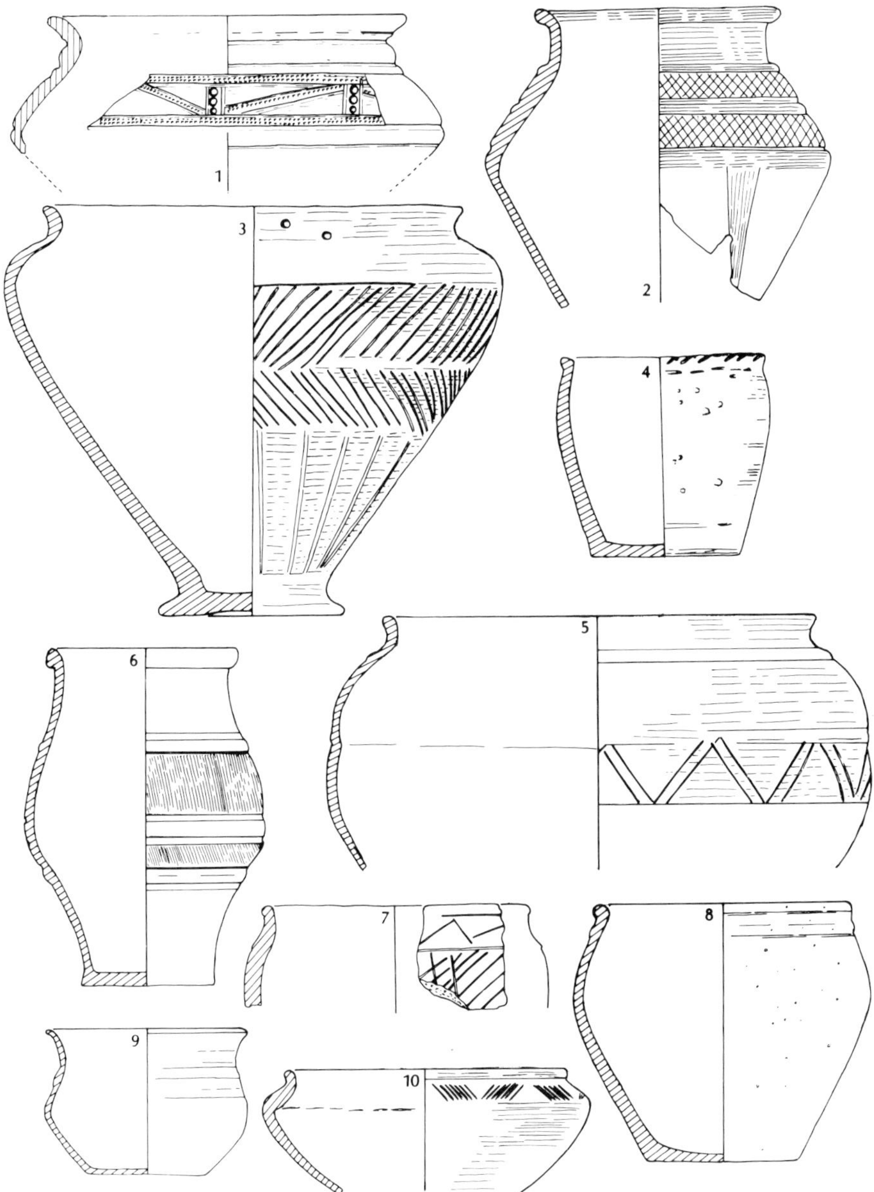

Figure 14. Very late pottery 1. 1, Old Sleaford, Lincolnshire (source, author). 2, Dragonby, South Humberside (source, author). 3, 5, 10, Danebury, Hampshire (after Cunliffe). 4, Moulton Park, Northamptonshire (after Williams). 6, 9, Aylesford, Kent (after Birchall). 7, Dunstan's Clump, Nottinghamshire (source, author). 8, Rampton, Nottinghamshire (source, author). To a scale of 1:4.

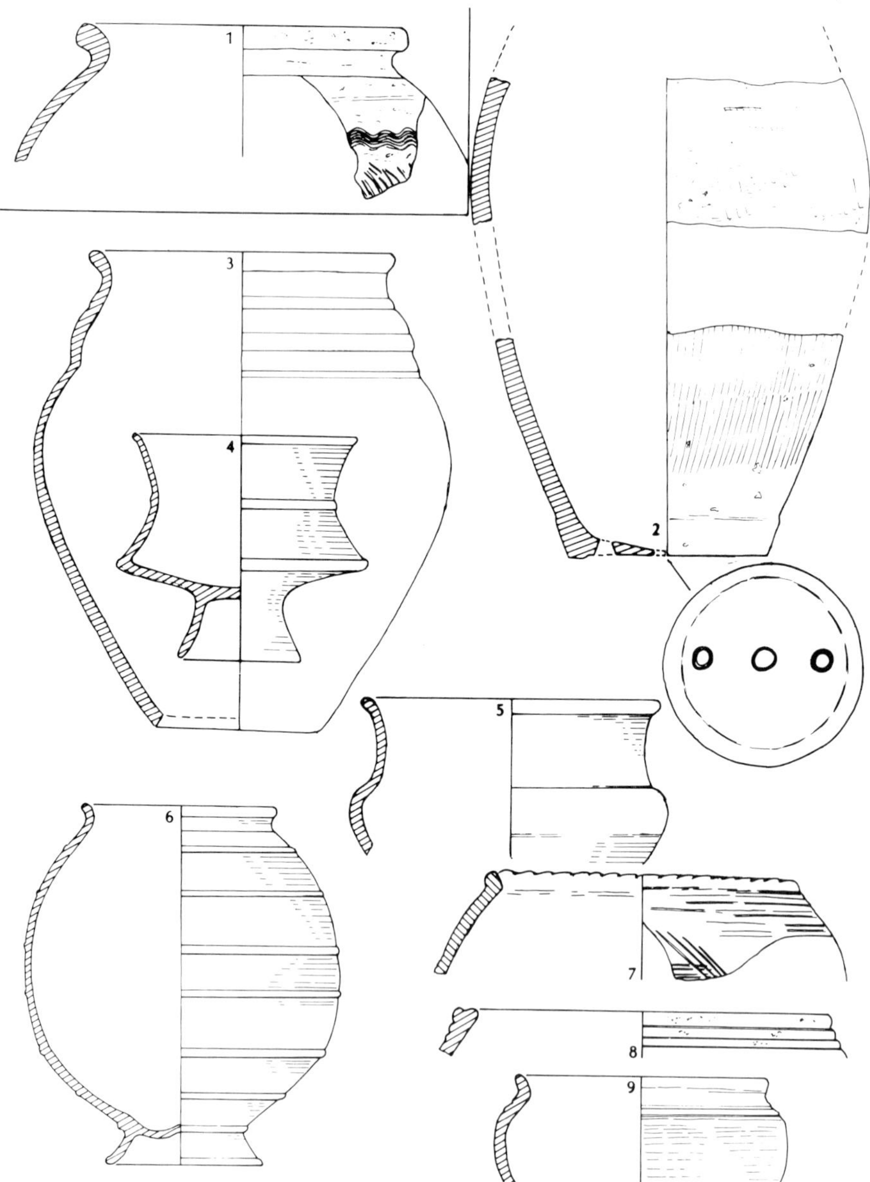

Figure 15. Very late pottery 2. 1, 3, Skeleton Green, Hertfordshire (after Rigby). 2, Old Sleaford, Lincolnshire (source, author). 4, Welwyn Garden City, Hertfordshire (after Stead). 5, 7, Baldock, Hertfordshire (after Rigby). 6, Hengistbury Head, Dorset (after Bushe-Fox). 8, 9, Carn Euny, Cornwall (source, author). To a scale of 1:4 (1, scale 1:8).

there are many pedestal bases and globular jars with slashed rims (**15**, 7). The grave at *Welwyn Garden City* arguably represents the peak of late iron age native pottery. Here there are pedestalled concave-sided bowls or *tazze* (**15**, 4), fine cordoned jars and beakers and imitation Gallo-Belgic platters, all in fine black polished ware.

The late Cornish pottery is dominated by the cordoned wares. Some, as in the example from Carn Euny, have a groove in the top of the rim (**15**, 8) while others have tapering out-turned rims (**15**, 9).

In the lowland areas the standard forms of pottery which have been described can be used confidently as dating evidence, both comparatively within and between sites and, to a lesser extent, as absolute evidence. Such use for dating becomes more problematical where pottery does not exhibit these standard forms, modifies them, or where there are mixed deposits. This is the common problem of the marginal areas between the more developed lowland zone and culturally poor upland Britain. These intermediate conditions are found in Nottinghamshire, where fine late decorated ware is missing altogether, but the typical cordons (albeit reduced to one or two) still occur on the necks of rather crude jars, as at *Rampton* (**14**, 8). Mixed deposits from such areas pose a slightly different dating problem: what is to be made of just one iron age pot with a neck cordon and an organised incised pattern found at *Dunston's Clump*, Nottinghamshire, a largely Roman rural site (**14**, 7)? The crude hand-made jars (**14**, 4) which occur together with concave-sided bowls at *Moulton Park*, near Northampton, can be dated with the help of these easily recognised bowls. But on many rural and upland zone sites only the crude pottery occurs, and this is almost impossible to date with any certainty. It can be immediately pre-conquest, contemporary with the first centuries of occupation, or even later. Only the luck of additional dating evidence, as at *Roxby* on the North Yorkshire Moors, enables such pottery to be pinpointed, in this case to immediately before the Roman conquest. This pottery, in effect, illustrates the unchanging and enforced conservatism of the poor; where the struggle for existence was greatest the iron age continued unaffected by the refinements of lowland Britain. Caesar tells of the 'tribes of the interior who do not grow corn but live on milk and meat and wear skins'.

Plate 9. Very late period. 'Belgic' pottery from Essex: (above, from left to right) Colchester bowl; pedestal urns from Cruksea and Lexden, Colchester; (below, from left to right) concave-sided bowl from Ardleigh; jar from Heybridge; bowl from Lexden, Colchester. (Colchester and Essex Museum.)

8
Decoration on later pottery

In the later pre-Roman iron age in lowland Britain certain decorative traits and motifs emerge which vary geographically. These flourish in the middle and late periods but disappear in the very latest one. This has been noted above in the descriptions of regional pottery types, but the decoration suggests other differences and wider influences. The motifs are all derived, in one way or another, from continental La Tène sources. The patterns concerned appear on both metalwork and pottery and are spread all over Europe, though with regional variations which provide evidence for links. Thus in Britain patterns in the south-west suggest close contacts with Armorica (Brittany) while in the east different interpretations strongly suggest derivation through trade via the Rhine.

The fabrics of the pottery vary from place to place and Dr D. P. S. Peacock has shown from petrological studies of south-western pottery that some pottery was made in restricted and identifiable areas. The best example is his group 1, made from gabbroic clay found only in the Lizard peninsula of Cornwall, which supplied an area at least 100 km across. Other groups based on fabrics with old red sandstone, calcite and shell inclusions supplied the Somerset area and some decorative techniques can be linked to postulated production centres there. This suggests groups of workshops using common sources of clay. It is not surprising that some of these groups developed common decorative traits. Peacock's group 2, for instance, based on old red sandstone from the Quantock Hills, seems to have supplied the lake villages of Meare and Glastonbury, which have a very distinctive style of decoration.

The exterior colour of all decorated vessels is usually black or very dark grey and, when it is lighter, tinged with brown. The outer surface, where preserved, is usually evenly burnished with a flat-ended tool about 2 to 3 mm across, but only sometimes are individual tool marks visible. The interiors are sometimes burnished for about 1 cm from the top of the rim.

The tools used for decoration were made from wood or bone and some of them, with circular carvings, have been preserved at Glastonbury. Others, now lost, were very carefully carved with concentric circular stamps and notched circlets. Roulette wheels (probably like pastry wheels) were also used, and an engraver with a U-shaped end. The impressions must have been made when the pots were leather-hard as there are no rough edges or burrs which would have resulted if the work had been done on wet clay.

Very broadly speaking, in eastern England patterns are geometric. They are based on arcs, interlocking arcs, triangles and chevrons. In the south-west scroll and triskele patterns predominate, but throughout the lowland zone there is a common stock of lozenge and triangle motifs. In the south-west reserved zones are hatched or filled with diagonal lines, whereas in Lincolnshire these areas are highly burnished. Generally the decoration is in zones, which are confined by tooled lines above and below. It is usually placed on the shoulder. All-over decoration is rare as, in the absence of tables, these vessels were presumably placed on the ground and viewed from above. Often the bases of foot-ring jars have a form of cross decoration, presumably seen when they were placed upside down to dry or when stored. All the patterns incorporate a range of circular stamps. These are usually placed singly or, in eastern areas, in groups of three.

The richest sites for decorated pottery are the lake villages of Meare and Glastonbury in Somerset, where the typical patterns were first recognised in the late nineteenth century. Here necked bowls and jars, barrel and saucepan pots have elaborate scroll patterns, which can be combined with simple circular stamps, and the reserve zones are often hatched (**17**, 2, 3). There are also triangle patterns and interlocking or nested chevrons alternately filled with diagonal lines (**16**, 3). Combinations of these with circular stamps produce patterns like the saltire (**17**, 4). Bases are decorated with interlocking arcs and triskeles (**17**, 8).

In Cornwall the patterns are simpler arcs and chevrons (**17**, 1) but scroll patterns do appear late in the sequence at *Carloggas*. Diagonal lines usually make up the background filling and this is rouletted in some of the earlier examples (**7**, 1, 2).

A feature of the central area of England is the dotted technique both for the main lines of the pattern and for background infilling. It is also used to accentuate the tooled patterns. Decoration is in plain bands of diagonal lines, simple arcs or chevrons with only a few circular stamps (**17**, 5, 6; **7**, 3, 5, 6).

In the Chiltern area, and extending north-east into Northamptonshire, globular bowls bear elaborate patterns. These are exceptional as the whole surface area is decorated in two zones.

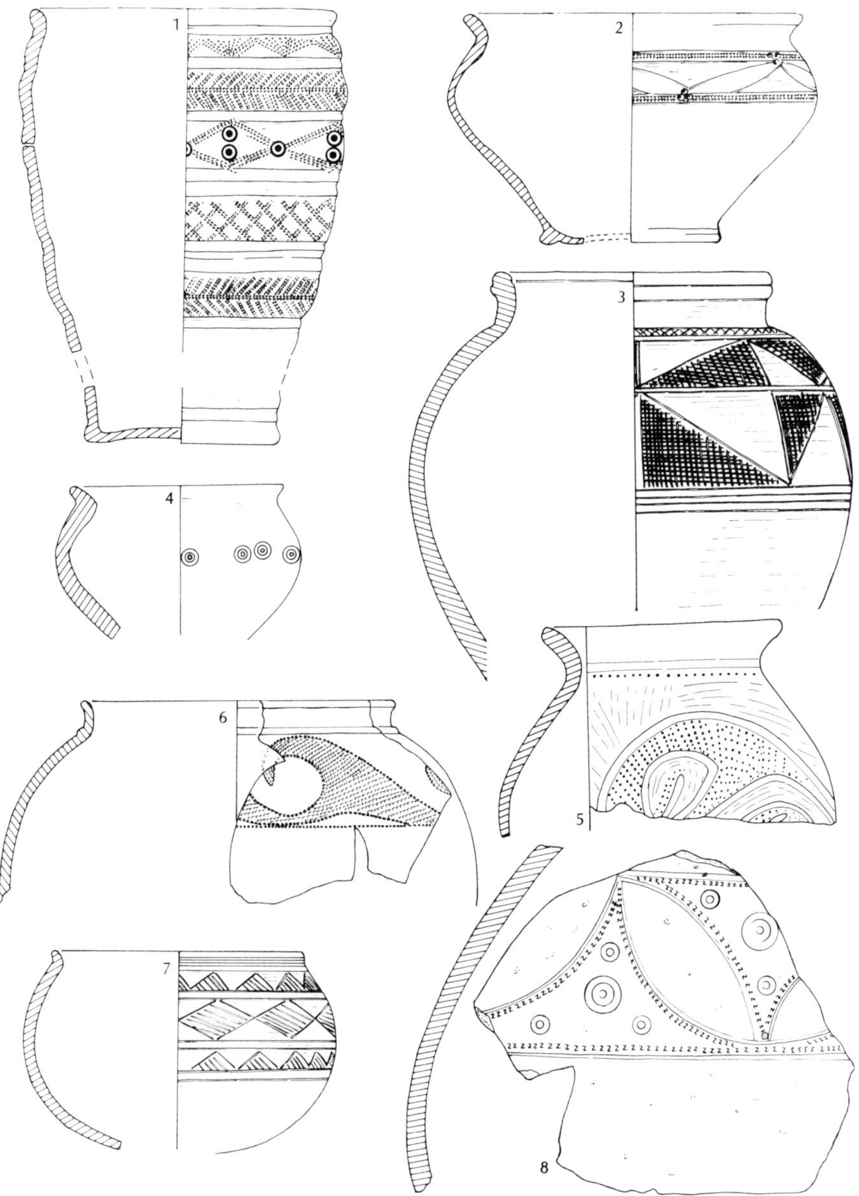

Figure 16. Decorated pottery. 1, Dragonby, South Humberside (source, author). 2, Old Sleaford, Lincolnshire (source, author). 3, Glastonbury, Somerset (after Bulleid and Gray). 4, Crayford, Kent (source, author). 5, Margate, Kent (source, author). 6, Hengistbury Head, Dorset (source, author). 7, Hunsbury, Northamptonshire (after Harding). 8, Nor Marsh, Kent (source, author). To a scale of 1:4 (8, scale 1:2).

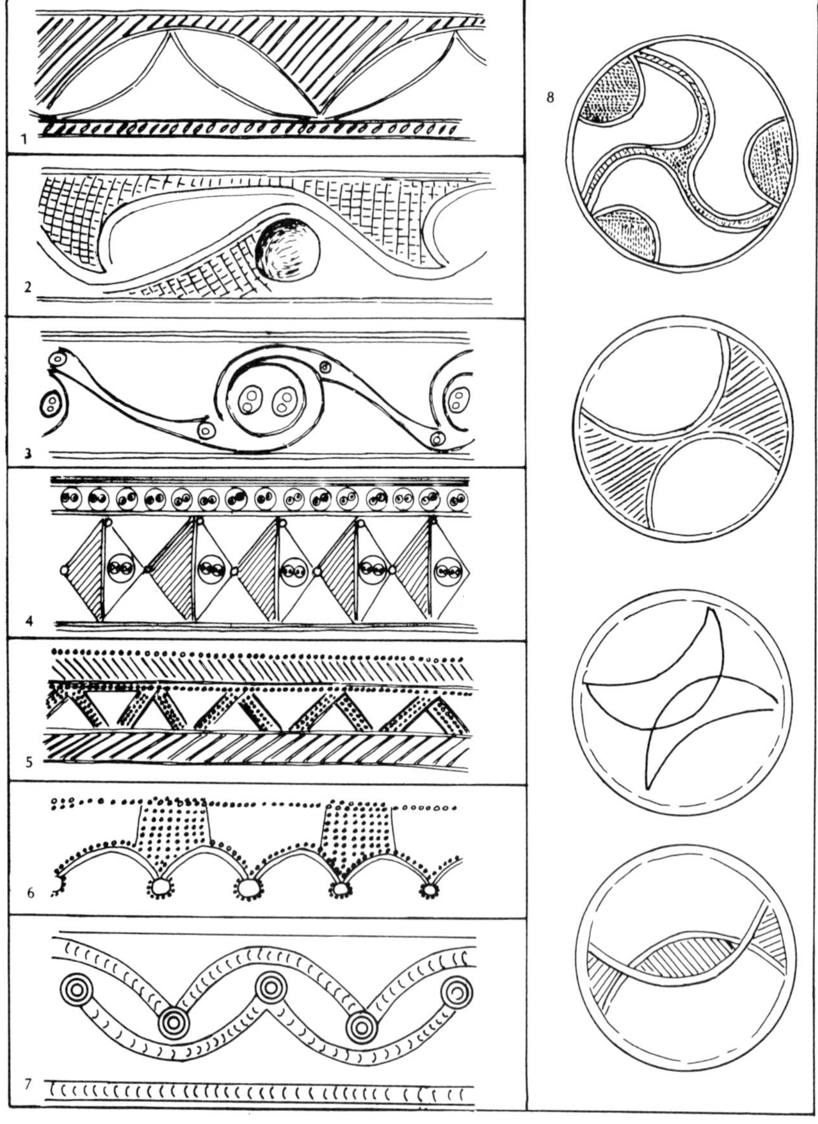

Figure 17. Decorative motifs in western Britain. 1, Carloggas, Cornwall. 2, 3, 4, Glastonbury, Somerset. 5, Danebury, Hampshire. 6, Yarnbury, Wiltshire. 7, Frilford, Oxfordshire. 8, Patterns on the underside of foot-ring bases at Meare and Glastonbury, Somerset.

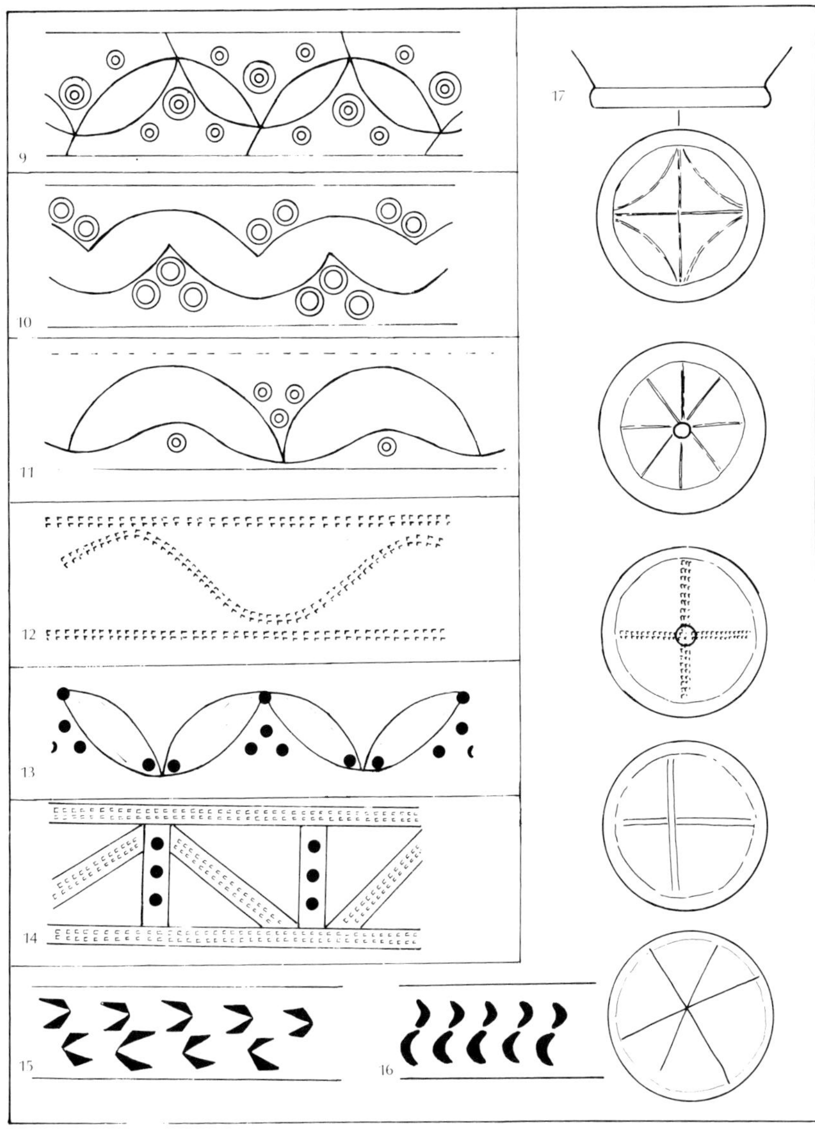

Figure 18. Decorative motifs in eastern Britain. 9, Canewdon, Essex. 10, Mucking, Essex. 11, Canewdon, Essex. 12, 13, Dragonby, South Humberside. 14, Ancaster, Lincolnshire. 15,16, Stamps on coarse ware jars from Dragonby, South Humberside. 17, Patterns on the underside of foot-ring bases from Dragonby.

In Oxfordshire the patterns are interlocking arcs combined with circular stamps and dotted decoration between double tooled lines (**17**, 7), while in Northamptonshire there are scroll patterns or filled triangles (**10**, 8, 9; **16**, 7).

The Thames estuary region has very elaborate interlocking arc patterns combined with double and triple concentric-circle stamps usually placed in groups of three. The lines of the pattern are simply tooled and the interest is in the arrangement and rearrangement of the arcs. Figures **18**, 9-11, and **9**, 3 and 4, illustrate the Celtic love of taking a pattern to pieces and then reassembling it in a different way. The same thing happened with coins, which were modelled on a gold stater of Philip of Macedon but are almost unrecognisable as such by the time they reach Britain. Stamps are sometimes used on their own in the area of the Thames estuary (**16**, 4). Two other examples of decoration from this area are illustrated on pots from *Margate* and from *Nor Marsh*, Kent, on the south side of the estuary (**16**, 5, 8).

Lincolnshire also has a very distinct style of decoration. Here the main lines of the pattern are usually rouletted with a double square-notched wheel and the reserve zones are burnished. This pattern burnishing is an unusual feature and can occur on its own without rouletting. On earlier pottery the patterns are often free rouletted ones (**18**, 12; **8**, 4). Most patterns combine rouletting and burnishing with circular stamps, singly and in groups of three (**18**, 13). The cross decorations on the bases are common to eastern parts of England and are less elaborate than the ones from Glastonbury (**18**, 17). In Lincolnshire they are sometimes

Plate 10. Very late period. Small-necked bowl from Dragonby, South Humberside. (Scunthorpe Borough Museum. Photograph: P. Dixon.)

Plate 11. Decorated sherds from Dragonby, South Humberside. (Above left) Double-rowed, square-notched rouletting and circular stamps. (Photograph: S. M. Elsdon.) (Above right) Pattern burnishing in interlocking arcs with dimple stamps. (Photograph: W. T. Jones.) (Below left) Stamps on coarse ware jars. (Photograph: W. T. Jones.) (Below right) Concentric circle and rosette stamps. (Photograph: S. M. Elsdon.)

rouletted. Rectilinear patterns such as in figure **18**, 14, are less common in the northern parts of the area than in the south, where they are common on necked bowls, for example figure **14**, 1. Another difference between the north and south of Lincolnshire is in the double tooled lines which accompany the rouletted lines. In the north the rouletting is on one side and in the south it is enclosed between the lines. These differences may denote different workshops. Two especially fine examples come from each of these areas: one unique example from *Dragonby* in the north is decorated all over (**16**, 1) and the second, also unique, is from *Old Sleaford* in the south (**11**, 1).

The only other site where rouletting is used for the main decoration is *Hengistbury Head* in Dorset. Here a group of large jars has both arc and key patterns in this technique, but in this location they might well be direct continental imports (**16**, 6).

Stamped decoration is not entirely confined to fine wares, as some late coarse jars have a single flat cordon with crude crescentic or triangular stamps.

Figure 19. Methods of firing.

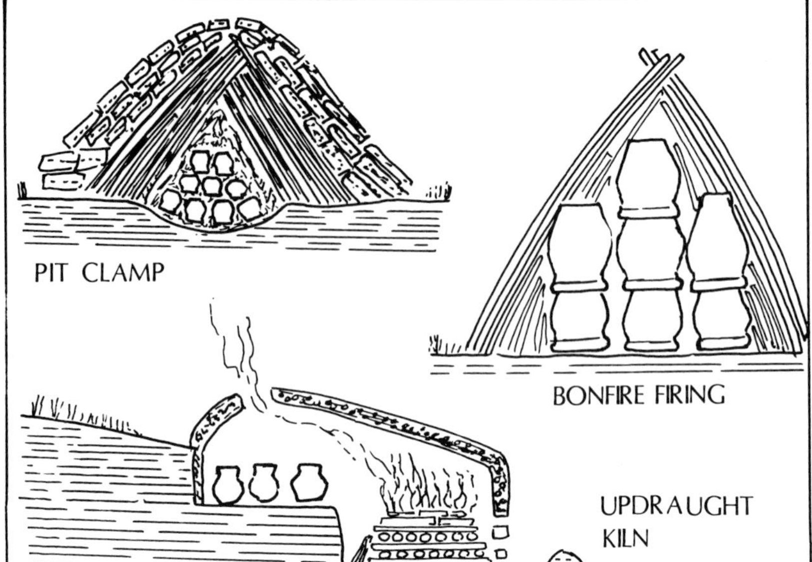

9
Methods of manufacture

Most British iron age pottery is hand-made. It is made by two methods and in both the clay must be kept wet. The first is to start with a ball of clay, into which the thumb is inserted and the sides are gradually pulled out to make the shape of the pot. The second is to make a flat base and then to roll the clay into sausages, which are joined to the base in coils to form the walls of the pot. The walls are then smoothed with thumb and fingers. It is possible that the walls of some larger pots were made by adding rolled-out slabs of clay to the flat bases.

The way in which a pot was made can usually be discovered through careful observation. Thumb pots have their own distinctive shape and finger impressions. Sometimes the coil method can be detected by diagonal breaks in the walls or by the shape of the coils themselves. This method was used for larger jars and it is possible to produce very large jars in this way, such as the huge Cretan storage jars of the Mediterranean bronze age. All hand-made pots are thicker at the shoulder than the neck, where breakages often occur. Round bases are formed either on a curved mould before the walls of the vessel are added, or by pushing out the flat base from inside when the pot is leather-hard.

Wheel-made pots tend to be much more even and often preserve the distinctive finger marks produced by a rapidly spinning wheel. Some pots can be seen to be hand-made except for the rim, which was probably finished on a slow wheel or turntable. There are distinct finger impressions on the inside of the shoulders, yet the rim is perfectly even. The first slow wheels were probably simple turntables on a pivot. None survives but there are one or two large reel-like objects of baked clay. These are called *tournettes* and it is assumed they were used for finishing and decorating hand-made pottery. Fast wheels could have had some kind of a heavy flywheel. Wheel-made pottery could have started as early as 30 BC in some parts of southern England, while further north *c.*10-1 BC is probably a more accurate date.

In temperate climates it was impossible to dry the clay completely before firing, therefore raw clay always had a filler of crushed flint, shell or stone added to it. The filler absorbs the heat of the fire faster than the clay and helps to keep the fabric open until the last drops of moisture evaporate. In this way the risk of pots exploding during firing is reduced. The types of filler used can help determine the origin of the pots as local material was used, for instance flint in the chalk areas of the south and fossil shell in areas of Jurassic limestone.

Formerly understanding of primitive methods of producing and firing pottery was based on comparison with methods still in use in underdeveloped parts of the world. This has now been supplanted by evidence from many experimental firings, especially those at the Iron Age Experimental Farm at Butser Hill in Hampshire. It is widely assumed that the pit clamp method of firing was used. For this a shallow depression was scooped out of the ground and lined with dry clay or straw and the pots were piled in to form a pyramid. Twigs were then packed around them and the whole pile was covered with green timber. Two cracks were left in the timber cover on either side to give access to the straw at the bottom for lighting. Fresh-cut turves were then piled around the heap of fuel and the fire was lit. Once the fire was fully ignited, more turves were piled on and any gaps filled with soil. This method ensured slow heating and prevented too much oxygen being drawn in as the temperature increased. If that happened the clamp oxidised and the pots turned red. Clay properly fired by the pit clamp method is reduced and the pots are black to dark brown in colour. Temperatures of 600 to 700 Celsius or more can be obtained in these clamps. They were not opened until they were quite cold, to prevent the finished pots oxidising when exposed to the air.

By the mid first century AD the first kilns were in use. These were simple updraught kilns usually built on a slope. The pottery was placed on a shelf and the fire built below it. A clay dome with a chimney was built over both shelf and firing chamber. When temperatures in the kiln reached 700 Celsius, or the pots glowed red, the door to the firing chamber was closed. Then either everything could be covered to produce black reduced pottery, or the chimney could be left open to draw in the oxygen as it cooled, which produced the red oxidised pottery that appears at the very end of the iron age. There is evidence in Northamptonshire for such kilns and portable kiln furniture was used. At Camp Hill, near Northampton, these kilns appear in the ground on excavation as burnt oval hollows with one steeper side.

It seems probable that some large storage jars were fired in an open bonfire. The green pots were placed upside down on the ground and piled one on top of the other. A fire was built round them and lit. Thus they are black inside and on the lower body, which the oxygen could not reach, while the top half is red.

10
Processing pottery and understanding reports

Pottery from excavation sites is always dirty and often comes in very large quantities. It will arrive from the site in trays, each labelled according to the particular feature or layer within a feature in which it was found. On an iron age site the bulk of the pottery will be body sherds of coarse, undistinguished ware but all must be carefully preserved. No attempt must be made to sort it at this stage and the first task, often done on the site, is to wash it carefully and clean the broken edges with a soft toothbrush. This will make sticking together sherds of the same pot easier at a later stage. When the pottery is thoroughly dry, each sherd is marked in indelible ink with a unique code number which will enable it to be related back instantly to the particular layer in which it was found, even if it should get separated from the rest of the context. A sherd without a mark is virtually useless in the interpretation of a site. Great care must therefore be taken at this stage. When the sherds are dry and marked, each group is put in separate transparent plastic bags and plainly labelled. All this is very painstaking and time-consuming but essential for interpretation by the specialist.

The first job for the specialist is to study each bag in detail. It is necessary to find out if all the sherds are made of the same material or if different fabrics are represented within the group. The pottery is then weighed and the number of sherds counted according to fabric (see below). All this is then listed according to weight by fabric and the number and proportion of rims, bases and handles present. The different fabrics are usually assessed in hand-held specimens at this stage, first by eye and then at about ten times magnification. Only when all this has been done will the pottery be spread out on tables according to features and layers. As each sherd has an individual mark it is now possible to move them around if joins or pieces of the same pot are suspected in different features. Only at this stage does it become possible to visualise the pottery from the site as a whole and its development, if any. A group of pottery from one set of features, a hut perhaps, might be quite different from the rest and so either early or late in the site's history. Another group might consist solely of coarse ware: this might indicate an area where food was stored in large jars. Joins between sherds which come from different layers or features may be found. These will tell the excavator that he can amalgamate the features in his notes. Some sherds, from a ditch for instance, may be very small and abraded, which would indicate that the ditch had been re-dug many times. A pottery specialist can, in this way, begin to tell the excavator much more about his site and the people who lived there than just the date and types of pottery.

The next stage is to draw all the interesting sherds, profiles, rims, bases and decoration and to arrange them according to features and period. Rim and base sherds are placed on a diameter chart and in this way it is possible to reconstruct pot profiles from rim sherds as small as 3 cm with a high degree of accuracy. So there is now a visual image of the development of the site in terms of the forms of pottery and types of decoration.

When the main pottery fabric types have been established, they are studied with the aid of a microscope. A 10 times magnification will give a good impression of the clay and types of inclusions, while 20 to 35 times can usually identify inclusions. A few selected samples will then be studied in thin sections of 30 microns (1 micron = 0.001 mm) so that a geologist can identify the minerals precisely. In this way the sources of both clay and fillers can be identified. As it is unlikely that raw clay would have been carried very far, it is now possible to say whether the pots were made locally or imported. It is very difficult to be certain whether or not a fine vessel is hand-made or wheel-made. Here, too, thin sections can sometimes help, especially if they are cut obliquely into the pot. If most of the particles in the clay matrix can be seen to have one orientation, it is likely that this was caused by manufacture on a fast wheel.

The pottery section of an excavation report will set out first the main fabrics and forms and will then relate these to the features. There will be illustrations of selected groups of pottery, followed by a typology for the site. This should explain clearly which pottery forms are associated with which group of structures and suggest a progression. For example, it might be possible to state that in the early phase there were three round houses which were lived in, three used for stock and a small enclosure ditch. In the second phase there might be six occupied houses with four structures for stock and an enlarged enclosure ditch. Structures for stock would contain very little pottery and no hearth. All this can be ascertained from carefully documented site evidence in which study of the pottery plays a vital part.

The data from the particular site now have to be related to and compared with others in the immediate region and further afield. This is important in order to assess the site's position in the wider environment and possibly to provide dating evidence.

When all this has been done the specialist can return to the excavator and request radiocarbon dates to establish certain key features, perhaps those at the beginning of the occupation of the site or in some important phase which can be linked to other, previously undated ones within the region. If radiocarbon dates are available for these features, then perhaps a new piece can be added to the jigsaw and a previously uncertain date be established or reinforced.

Some of the pottery we find is extremely well made with a skill not exceeded by later generations despite improved technology. Nevertheless, sometimes very dirty and often small undistinguished sherds, from either excavations or field walking, can have a great potential which we cannot afford to ignore. All of it has a story to tell of the people who made it if only we ask the right questions.

11
Glossary

Cabling (applied cordons): strips of clay applied to the surface of a pot for decorative purposes. Finger impressions in the cordons give them the appearance of cables.

Countersunk handles: normally handles are made separately and attached to the vessel. In this method, however, a small eyelet handle is formed by pinching a thickened portion of the shoulder so that one side of the eyelet is a cavity in the profile of the vessel.

Filler: non-clay material in the fabric of a pot, which has been added to prevent damage during firing.

Haematite: a reddish brown colouring derived from a mineral containing iron ore. It is used for decorating the surface of some pottery.

Inclusion: naturally occurring non-clay material (minerals and so on) in the fabric of a pot.

Omphalos: literally, a navel; a circular depression in the base of a pot.

Oppidum: a Latin word used for a late iron age town which is usually, but not always fortified. Plural: oppida.

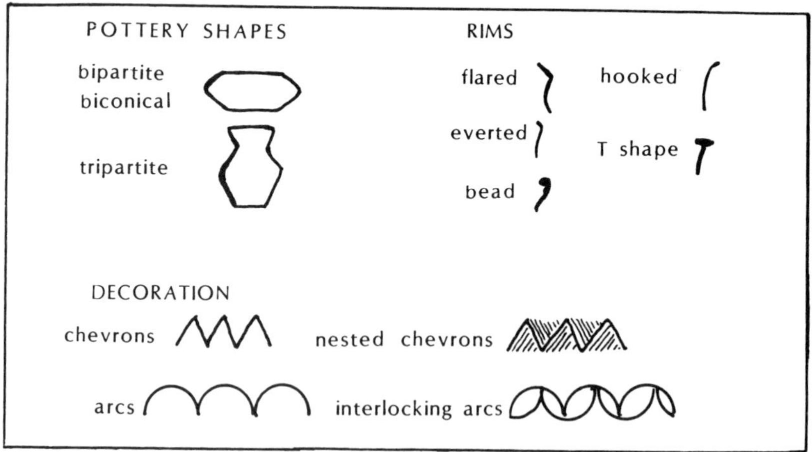

Figure 20. Terms used in pottery descriptions.

Radiocarbon dating: a technique which assesses the amount of radioactive carbon-14 (present in all living organisms) remaining in organic material. As the rate of decay of carbon-14 is known, the date of an archaeological sample can be determined by measuring the residual amount of radioactivity. But because carbon-14 has been affected by fluctuations in background atmospheric radiation levels, the dates can never be exact and are expressed with a ± symbol.

Reserved zone: an area set apart by decoration in some way such as hatching, rouletting or burnishing.

Rilling: narrow, closely placed horizontal grooves.

Rouletting: decoration made by a square-notched wheel or some other kind of wheel, as on butt beakers.

Saltire: a decorative motif; see central panel of figure **17**, 4.

Situlate: a word used to describe a large pottery jar with high shoulders. A *situla* is a bucket-shaped vessel of sheet bronze. Examples from the north Italian iron age were particularly elaborately decorated.

Slip: a solution of liquid clay into which a pot is dipped, before firing, to give it a fine surface.

Tazza: an angular goblet-shaped vessel of the late iron age (see **15**, 4). Plural: *tazze*.

Temper: see *Filler* above; alternative terminology.

Triskele: a decorative motif; three legs or arcs radiating from a common centre; see **17**, 8.

Wasters: pots which have become distorted during firing and have presumably been discarded near the place of manufacture.

12
Museums

Andover Museum and Museum of the Iron Age, 6 Church Close, Andover, Hampshire SP10 1DP. Telephone: 0264 66283. Excellent display of local iron age material, particularly from Danebury hillfort.

Ashmolean Museum of Art and Archaeology, Beaumont Street, Oxford OX1 2PH. Telephone: 0865 278000. Important collections from Oxfordshire and the Thames valley; also Aylesford, Kent, and Rainsborough, Northamptonshire.

Brighton Art Gallery and Museum, Church Street, Brighton, East Sussex. Telephone: 0273 603005. Late bronze age material from Plumpton Plain and iron age material from Cissbury Camp and Saltdean.

British Museum, Great Russell Street, London WC1B 3DG. Telephone: 01-636 1555. 1000 to 600 BC: a good selection of domestic material from sites in Kent, Essex, North Yorkshire and Humberside. A gap from 600 to 50 BC and then excellent material from Welwyn Garden City and a selection of pedestal jars and tazze from burials in Bedfordshire, Hertfordshire and Kent. Very good displays of continental pottery from Urnfield (bronze age), Hallstatt and La Tène I periods.

Butser Ancient Farm Demonstration Area, Queen Elizabeth Country Park, near Petersfield, Hampshire. Telephone: 0705 598838. Experimental reconstruction of iron age farming settlement.

Cambridge University Museum of Archaeology and Anthropology, Downing Street, Cambridge CB2 3DZ. Telephone: 0223 337733 or 333516. Good collection of East Anglian material from late bronze age to first century AD.

Castle Museum, Norwich, Norfolk NR1 3JU. Telephone: 0603 611277 extension 24. Important groups of pottery from West Harling and Cromer.

Cheltenham Art Gallery and Museum, Clarence Street, Cheltenham, Gloucestershire GL50 3JT. Telephone: 0242 237431. Material from local iron age hillforts, especially Salmondsbury and Cleeve Hill.

Colchester and Essex Museum, The Castle, Colchester, Essex CO1 1TJ. Telephone: 0206 712490. Good display of Belgic pottery from Essex graves such as Lexden, Braintree. A little south-eastern B Crayford-type pottery.

Cornwall County Museum, River Street, Truro, Cornwall TR1 2SJ. Telephone: 0872 72205. Comprehensive collection of Cornish material and displays from Castle Dore, Chysauster, Carloggas and Porthmeor.

Devizes Museum, 41 Long Street, Devizes, Wiltshire SN10 1NS. Telephone: 0380 77369. Material from All Cannings Cross.

Dorset County Museum, High West Street, Dorchester, Dorset DT1 1XA. Telephone: 0305 62735. Major exhibit on Maiden Castle and on the farming settlement of Gussage All Saints.

Glastonbury Lake Village Museum, The Tribunal, High Street, Glastonbury, Somerset. Telephone: 0458 32949. Exhibition on Glastonbury lake village.

Letchworth Museum and Art Gallery, Broadway, Letchworth, Hertfordshire SG6 3PF. Telephone: 0462 685647. Pottery from Ravensburgh hillfort and an important late iron age collection from Baldock.

Museum of London, London Wall, London EC2Y 5HN. Telephone: 01-600 3699. Late bronze to early iron age pottery from Heathrow.

Museum of Sussex Archaeology, Barbican House, 169 High Street, Lewes, East Sussex BN7 1YE. Telephone: 0273 474379. Late bronze age material from Itford Hill and iron age material from Caburn, Trundle, Little Horsted and other sites.

Northampton Central Museum and Art Gallery, Guildhall Road, Northampton NN1 1DP. Telephone: 0604 37413. Pottery from Hunsbury hillfort on display and a comprehensive collection of local material in store.

Nottingham University Museum, Department of Archaeology, The University, Nottingham NG7 2RD. Telephone: 0602 484848 extension 2564. Good collection of local material and a display from Dragonby, South Humberside.

Passmore Edwards Museum, Romford Road, Stratford, London E15 4LZ. Telephone: 01-519 4296. Good collection of material from southern Essex, including Mucking and the hillfort of Danbury.

Peterborough City Museum and Art Gallery, Priestgate, Peterborough, Cambridgeshire PE1 1LF. Telephone: 0733 43329. Material from important fenland sites, particularly Fengate.

Prittlewell Priory, Priory Park, Victoria Avenue, Southend-on-Sea, Essex SS2 6EX. Telephone: 0702 342878. Late material from Canewdon and North Shoebury and early pots from Great Wakering.

Reading Museum and Art Gallery, Blagrave Street, Reading,

Berkshire RG1 1QH. Telephone: 0734 575911 extension 2242. Material from Blewburton hillfort and items dredged from the Thames and Kennet rivers. A meagre display but much material in store.

Red House Museum, Quay Road, Christchurch, Dorset BH23 1BU. Telephone: 0202 482860. Some material from early excavations at Hengistbury Head.

Scunthorpe Borough Museum and Art Gallery, Oswald Road, Scunthorpe, South Humberside DN15 7BD. Telephone: 0724 843533. Good display of local iron age pottery from Dragonby.

Sheffield City Museum, Weston Park, Sheffield, South Yorkshire S10 2TP. Telephone: 0742 768588. Comprehensive collection of material from the Peak District of Derbyshire and displays from Mam Tor and Harborough caves.

Somerset County Museum, Taunton Castle, Castle Green, Taunton, Somerset TA1 4AA. Telephone: 0823 255504. Small display from Meare and Glastonbury lake villages and a large quantity in store. Also some material from South Cadbury.

Towner Art Gallery and Local History Museum, Manor Gardens, High Street, Old Town, Eastbourne, East Sussex BN20 8BB. Telephone: 0323 21635 or 25112. Display of Hallstatt pottery from Eastbourne.

Worthing Museum and Art Gallery, Chapel Road, Worthing, West Sussex BN11 1HD. Telephone: 0903 39999 extension 121. Small display from Park Brow and Highdown. Local material in store.

13
Further reading

General works

Avery, M. 'British La Tène Decorated Pottery: An Outline', *Études Celtiques*, 13 (1973), 522-51.

Barrett, J. C. 'The Pottery of the Later Bronze Age in Lowland England', *Proceedings of the Prehistoric Society*, 46 (1980), 297-320.

Burgess, C. 'The Bronze Age', in C. Renfrew (editor), *British Prehistory: A New Outline*. Duckworth, 1974.

Caesar. *The Conquest of Gaul* (translated by S. A. Handford).

Penguin Books, 1970. A good description of the Britons on page 136.

Cunliffe, B. *Iron Age Communities in Britain*. Routledge and Kegan Paul, 1974.

Gibson, A. *Neolithic and Early Bronze Age Pottery*. Shire, 1986.

Grimes, W. F. 'Art on British Iron Age Pottery', *Proceedings of the Prehistoric Society*, 18 (1952), 160-75.

Harding, D. W. *The Iron Age in Lowland Britain*. Routledge and Kegan Paul, 1974.

Harding, D. W. *The Iron Age in the Upper Thames Basin*. Oxford University Press, 1972.

May, J. *Prehistoric Lincolnshire*. History of Lincolnshire Committee, Lincoln, 1976.

Megaw, J. V. S., and Simpson, D. D. A. *An Introduction to British Prehistory*. Leicester University Press, 1979. Good general sections on late bronze to late iron age metalwork and pottery.

Reynolds, P. J. *Farming in the Iron Age*. Cambridge University Press, Topic Book, 1976. Descriptions of pottery making and firing techniques.

Sites with important pottery reports

Alcock, L. 'The Cadbury Castle Sequence in the First Millennium BC', *Bulletin of the Board of Celtic Studies*, 28 (1980), 656-718.

Birchall, A. 'The Aylesford-Swarling Culture etc', *Proceedings of the Prehistoric Society*, 31 (1965), 241-367.

Bradley, R., and Ellison, A. *Rams Hill: a Bronze Age Defended Enclosure*. British Archaeological Reports, 19, Oxford, 1975.

Brewster, T. C. M. *The Excavation of Staple Howe*. East Riding Archaeological Research Committee, 1973.

Bulleid, A., and Gray, H. St G. *The Glastonbury Lake Village* (two volumes). Glastonbury Antiquarian Society, 1911 and 1917.

Bulleid, A., and Gray, H. St G. *The Meare Lake Village* (two volumes). Taunton, 1948 and 1953.

Burstow, G. P., and Holleyman, G. A. 'Late Bronze Age Settlement on Itford Hill, Sussex', *Proceedings of the Prehistoric Society*, 23 (1957), 167-212.

Chowne, P.; Girling, M.; and Greig, J. 'Excavations at an Iron Age Defended Enclosure at Tattershall Thorpe, Lincolnshire', *Proceedings of the Prehistoric Society*, 52 (1986), 159-88.

Clark, J. G. D., and Fell, C. I. 'An Early Iron Age Site at Micklemoor Hill, West Harling, Norfolk', *Proceedings of the Prehistoric Society*, 19 (1953), 1-40.

Coles, J. M. *Meare Village East. The Excavations of A. Bulleid and H. St George Gray 1932-1956*. Somerset Levels Papers, 13 (1987).

Coombes, D. G., and Thompson, F. H. 'Excavation of the Hill Fort of Mam Tor, Derbyshire', *Derbyshire Archaeological Journal*, 99 (1979), 7-51.

Cotton, M. A., and Frere, S. S. 'Ivinghoe Beacon Excavations, 1963-5', *Records of Buckinghamshire*, 18 (1968), 187-260.

Cunliffe, B. *Hengistbury Head*. Paul Eleck, 1978. Early and short version of the following.

Cunliffe, B. *Hengistbury Head, Dorset*, volume 1 '300 BC-AD 500'. Oxford University Committee for Archaeology, Monograph 13, 1978.

Cunliffe, B., and Phillipson, D. W. 'Excavations at Eldon's Seat, Encombe, Dorset', *Proceedings of the Prehistoric Society*, 34 (1968), 191-237.

Cunnington, M. E. *The Early Iron Age Inhabited Site at All Cannings Cross Farm, Wilts*. Devizes, 1923.

Dudley, D. 'An Excavation at Bodrifty, Mulfra Hill, near Penzance, Cornwall', *Archaeological Journal*, 113 (1956), 1-32.

Elsdon, S. M. *Stamp and Roulette Decorated Pottery of the La Tène Period in Eastern England*. British Archaeological Reports, 10, Oxford, 1975.

Fell, C. I. 'The Hunsbury Hill-Fort, Northants', *Archaeological Journal*, 93 (1936).

Hawkes, C. F. C., and Hull, M. R. *Camulodunum*. Report of the Research Committee of the Society of Antiquaries of London, 14 (1947).

Hüsson, C. M. *A Rich Late La Tène Burial at Hertford Heath, Hertfordshire*. British Museum Occasional Paper, 44 (1983).

Inman, R., *et al*. 'Roxby Iron Age Settlement etc', *Proceedings of the Prehistoric Society*, 51 (1985), 181-214.

Jackson, D. A. 'An Iron Age Site at Twywell, Northamptonshire', *Northamptonshire Archaeology*, 10 (1975), 31-93.

Kenyon, K. M. 'Excavations at Breedon-on-the-Hill, 1946', *Transactions of the Leicestershire Archaeological Society*, 26 (1950), 17-28.

Kenyon, K. M. 'Excavations at Sutton Walls, Herefordshire, 1948-51', *Archaeological Journal*, 110 (1953), 1-87.

Longley, D. *Runnymede Bridge 1976: Excavations on the Site of a*

Late Bronze Age Settlement. Research Volume of the Surrey Archaeological Society, 6 (1980).

Musson, C. R. 'Excavation at the Breiddin, 1969-73' in D. W. Harding (editor), *Hillforts and Later Prehistoric Earthworks in Britain and Ireland*. Academic Press, 1976.

Peacock, D. P. S. 'A Contribution to the Study of Glastonbury Ware from South Western Britain', *Antiquaries Journal*, 49 (1969), 41-62.

Powlesland, D., *et al*. 'Excavations at Heslerton, North Yorkshire, 1978-82', *Archaeological Journal*, 143 (1986), 53-173.

Prior, F. *Excavation at Fengate, Peterborough, England: Fourth Report*. Northamptonshire Archaeological Society, Monograph 2 (1984).

Radford, C. A. R. 'Report on the Excavations at Castle Dore', *Journal of the Royal Institute of Cornwall* (new series), 1 (1951), appendix.

Rigby, V. 'The Gallo-Belgic Wares', in C. Partridge (editor), *Skeleton Green. A Late Iron Age and Romano-British Site*. Britannia Monograph Series, 2 (1981), 159-95.

Stanford, S. C. *Midsummer Hill; an Iron Age Hillfort on the Malverns*. Hereford, 1981.

Stead, I. M. 'A La Tène III Burial at Welwyn Garden City', *Archaeologia*, 101 (1967), 1-62.

Stead, I. M., and Rigby, V. *Baldock. The Excavation of a Roman and Pre-Roman Settlement, 1968-72*. Britannia Monograph Series, 7 (1986).

Threipland, L. M. 'An Excavation at St Mawgan-in-Pydar, North Cornwall', *Archaeological Journal*, 113 (1956), 33-81.

Wheeler, R. E. M. *Maiden Castle, Dorset*. Oxford, 1943.

Wheeler, R. E. M., and Richardson, K. M. *Hillforts of Northern France*. Oxford, 1957.

Wheeler, R. E. M., and Wheeler, T. V. *Verulamium, A Belgic and Two Roman Cities*. Oxford, 1936.

Williams, J. H. *Two Iron Age Sites in Northamptonshire*. Northampton Development Corporation Archaeological Monographs, 1 (1974).

Woods, P. J. 'Types of Late Belgic and Early Romano-British Pottery Kilns in the Nene Valley', *Britannia*, 5 (1974), 262-81.

Worsfold, F. H. 'A Report on the Late Bronze Age Site Excavated at Minnis Bay, Birchington, Kent, 1938-1940', *Proceedings of the Prehistoric Society*, 9 (1943), 28-47.

Index

Page numbers in italic refer to illustrations